YO-ALK-103

of the Dance

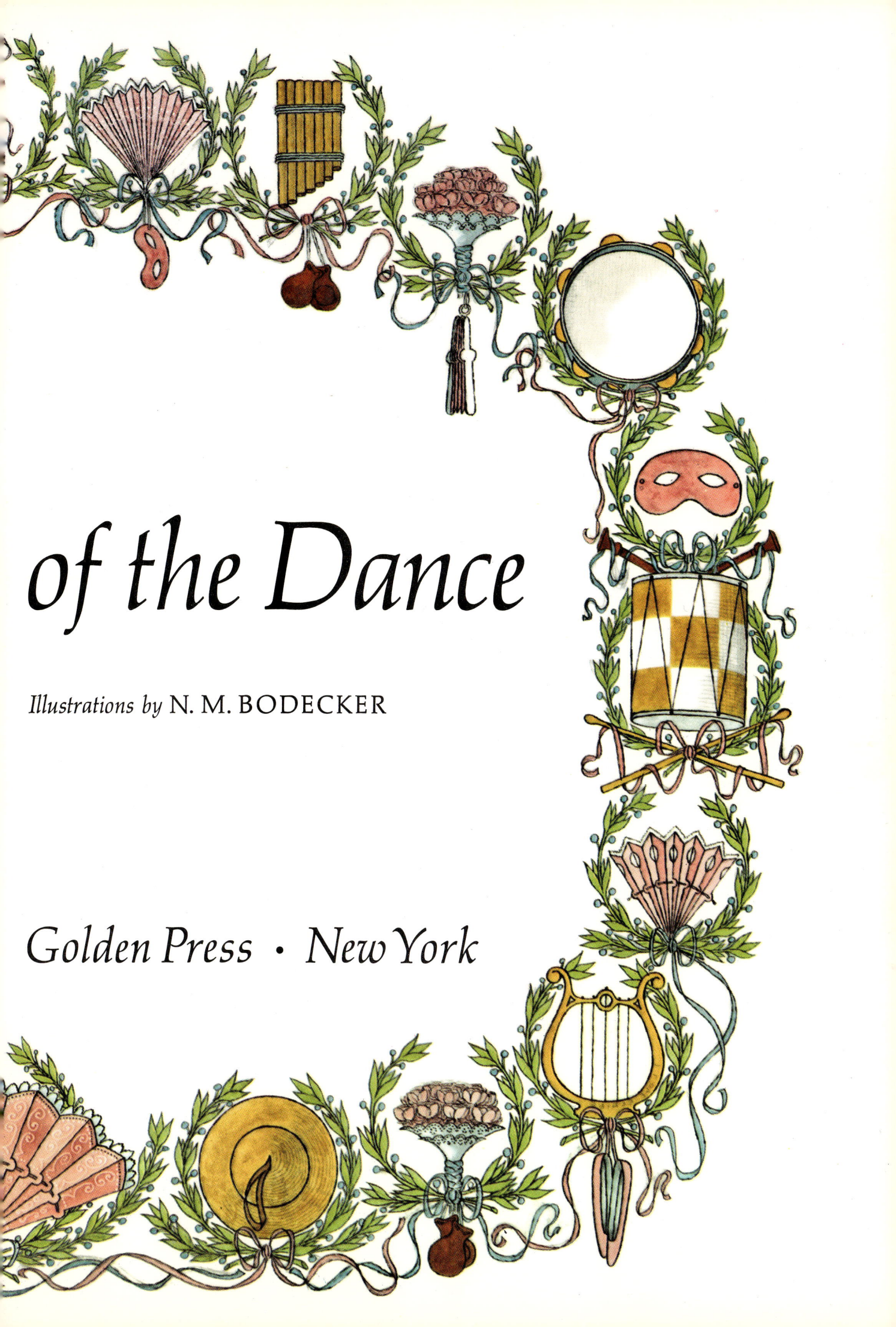

Illustrations by N. M. BODECKER

Golden Press · New York

TO
LILLY BESS CAMPBELL
PROFESSOR OF ENGLISH AND HISTORY OF THE DRAMA
UNIVERSITY OF CALIFORNIA
LOS ANGELES, CALIFORNIA

ACKNOWLEDGMENTS

The author wishes to thank the following experts
for their advice and help in collection of material:
Rudolf Wittkower, Professor of Art History, Columbia University;
Joseph Campbell, Member of the Faculty of Literature, Sarah Lawrence College;
May Gadd, Director, American Country Dance Society;
Alfred Opoku, Kumasi College of Technology, Ghana;
and Carl heinz Ostertag.

The author also wishes to express gratitude for permission
to use passages from *Fokine: Memoirs of a Ballet Master*,
by Vitale Fokine, published by Little, Brown & Company,
Copyright © 1961 by Vitale Fokine
and from the book *Theatre Street by* Tamara Karsavina.
Copyright, 1931, 1950, by E. P. Dutton & Co., Inc.,
renewal © 1959 by Tamara Karsavina.
Reprinted by permission of the publishers.

Photographs of pictures in the Collection of Lillian Moore
taken by Morris Leftoff, Green-Morris Studios

Isadora Duncan

LIBRARY OF CONGRESS CATALOG CARD NUMBER: 63-18908
©COPYRIGHT 1963 BY GOLDEN PRESS, INC.
DESIGNED AND PRODUCED BY ARTISTS AND WRITERS PRESS, INC.
PRINTED IN THE U.S.A. BY WESTERN PRINTING AND LITHOGRAPHING COMPANY.
PUBLISHED BY GOLDEN PRESS, INC., NEW YORK.
PUBLISHED SIMULTANEOUSLY IN CANADA BY
THE MUSSON BOOK COMPANY, LTD., TORONTO.

Arthur Mitchell and Diana Adams in Balanchine's Agon

Martha Swope Photo
New York City Ballet

Contents

BOOK I · RITUAL AND SOCIAL DANCE
Definitions 7
The Language of Dance 18
Types of Dances 23
The Development of Western Dance 32
Root Comparisons of East and West 48
The Moors in Spain 53
Medieval and Renaissance Dances 59
American Social Dances 66

BOOK II · THE THEATER AND BALLET
The Rise of the Western Theater 74
The Court Ballet 79
The First Great Ballet Dancers 93
The Golden Age 101
Ballet in America 119
The Decline 123
The American Music Halls 128
Duncan 135
Fokine 138
The Stars of the Diaghileff Ballet 147
The Revolutionists 156
Contemporary Folk Dance Groups 166
Contemporary Ballet 172
Contemporary American Ballet 188
Contemporary Ballet Stars 194

BOOK III · CHOREOGRAPHY
Composing Dances 203
Work Methods 209
The Principal Ballets of Influential Choreographers....245
Index 249

Book I

RITUAL AND SOCIAL DANCE

Definitions

WORKS OF ART are the symbols through which men communicate what lies beyond ordinary speech. Many people think of art as something special and apart from their daily lives, as a luxury, an occupation or hobby for impractical individuals. This is a mistake. Men cannot live without art. It is a necessity, as religion is. If men cannot communicate they die of loneliness. Art is communication on the deepest and most lasting level.

All of us need to tell what is in our hearts, but most of us manage to say what we really mean only at three or four high moments in our lifetime, and perhaps then only to intimates. The artist tries to reach anyone who will listen; but to do this he must talk through symbols.

The ability to convey or reproduce emotion gives great power; it is a tremendous gift, mysterious and precious. Men value emotion; it is one of the chief well-springs of human activity, but it is perishable. It lasts only a brief time and it can affect people only while it is strong. So artists try to fix it in forms that will endure and that will arouse a response in many people at widely different times.

Great art outlasts life, fashions, conditions, inventions, and all the changing circumstances of the world. Great art affects us as though the artist stood before us and spoke with the full force of living persuasion. Time and altered circumstance make absolutely no difference. We would not, for instance, understand one word an ancient Egyptian spoke were he to reappear and talk to us, but his sculptures convey emotion instantly and powerfully. It may not be exactly the emotion he wished to express; this we cannot know. The miracle is that the sculptures move us today in terms of our life and needs thousands of years after the hand that wrought them is gone. It reflects the color of subsequent lives and times; it has a life of its own. This is its strength.

This is true of all art, and it is true of dancing, which, because dependent on human habits and action, is the most malleable and changeable. It is also the oldest art. It is the mother or germinal form. Music came as an accompaniment to dance, and song as punctuation and comment. Ritual costume and masks, which are the beginning of theatrical impersonation, were first used in dance ceremonials. The theater is rooted in and grew out of ritual masked dancing.

Before man can do anything, he must draw breath, he must move. Movement is the source and condition of life.

The elements of dance are space, time, and human bodies.

Rhythmic beats and music are frequently used with dancing as aid and incitement, but dancing is an independent art and can exist without audible accompaniment.

Isadora Duncan in the Parthenon, 1921

Dancing is an arrangement or pattern in space, as architecture and painting are, and employs, as they do, spatial rhythm.

It is an arrangement in time, as music is, and employs time rhythm, as music does. Music consists of repeated patterns of accented and unaccented beats, which we call rhythm in time, and patterns or sequences of tone, which we call melody.

Dancing employs rhythm in both spheres—audible and visual. It is a time-space art, and the only one. Sometimes rhythm in space is particularly stressed, as in ballet dancing, and sometimes rhythm in time, as in Spanish and tap dancing. Dancing must always use both to some degree.

All Photos
United Press International

Dancing differs from all other exercise.
Sports require skill, coordination, and strength, but they are not dancing nor the stuff of dancing. Even when pleasing to watch, their real meaning lies in the practical results: the food caught, the game won, the record set.

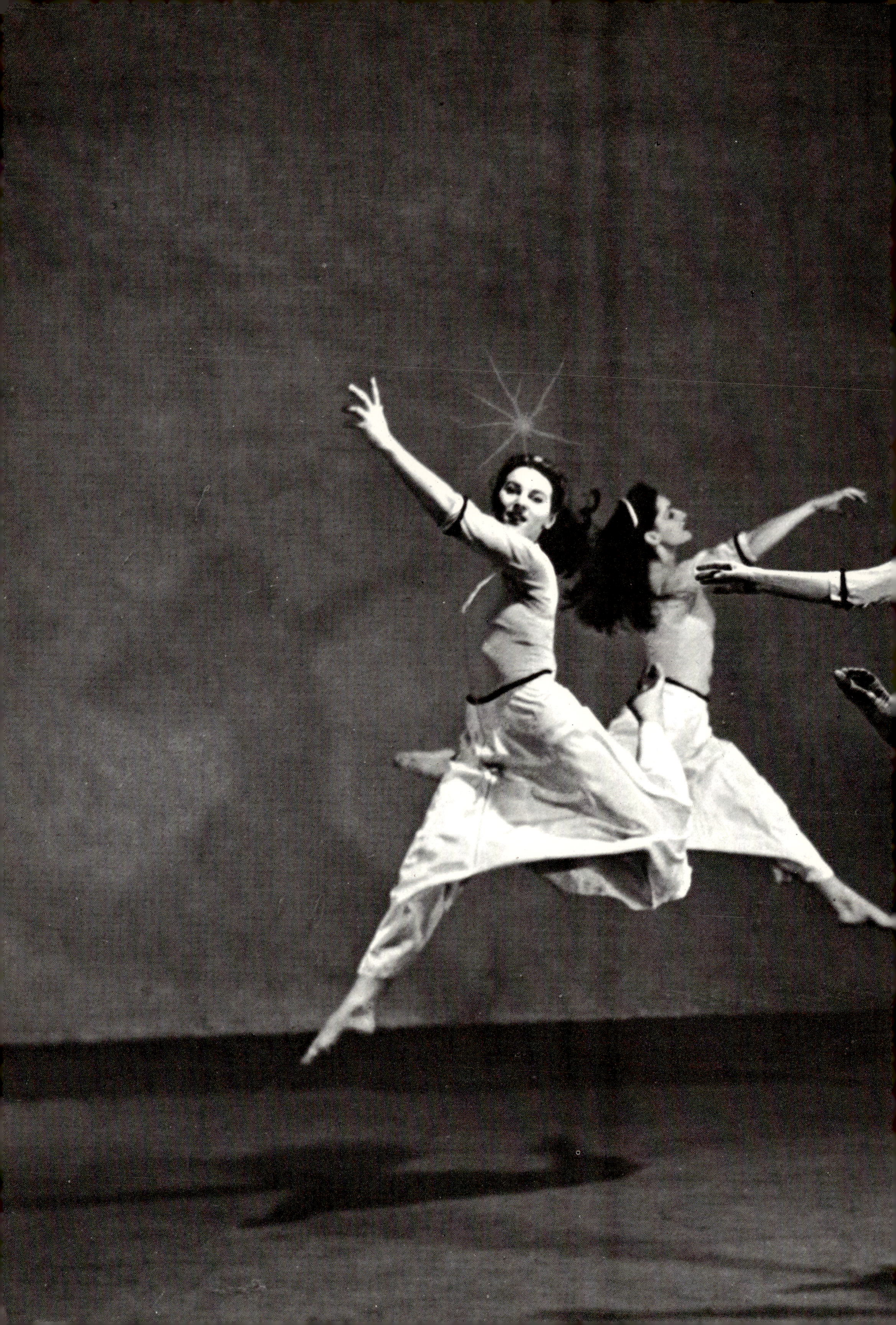

This is dancing.

Barbara Morgan Photo
from "Martha Graham" by B. Morgan,
pub. Duell, Sloan & Pearce

Fritz Peyer

Dancing moves us. It excites us. It compels or persuades us. It reveals to us aspects of life and human emotion.

Because we are in close physical sympathy with what we are looking at, dangerous stunts cause us to contract and tense our muscles and tighten our nerves. Free floating jumps give us the sense of flying. Physical difficulties surmounted with ease and joy exhilarate us. Rhythms set our blood racing and our feet tapping in sympathy. There is *pattern,* which sports do not have because they rely on chance and adventure. Uncertainty is their essence. Pattern is law. It makes a statement, a conclusion. And in dancing, it is through the pattern of steps that emotion is transmitted.

In all man-made design there is a conscious arrangement that stresses certain elements and discards others, that forces a point of view, that makes a statement. Certain harmonies and sequences make us weep; others make us laugh. It is the pattern that moves us in spite of our unfamiliarity with the subject matter or the performers. It is the pattern that effects a temporary "suspension of disbelief," that involves us emotionally with the artist and his intent.

Pattern is a planned arrangement of stresses and accents in repetition. In sound, a simple pattern would be beats on a drum in even time, with the first of every four accented.

We call this rhythm. Gravel going down a chute has no pattern or rhythm since there is no repetition of any recognizable arrangement. No idea is conveyed except gravel.

Form is the complete shape or map of a work. In a time art (music, literature, or dancing), it is the line or track that leads from the beginning through the middle or development to a satisfying and logical end. In a space art (architecture, painting, dancing), it is the satisfactory relation of the physical parts to the space in which they function and their interrelation.

Symmetry is a pattern that is alike on both sides of an axis. Symmetrical design tends to be restful and satisfying to watch.

Asymmetry is a pattern that is not alike on both sides. Asymmetrical design is disturbing and exciting.

Jack Mitchell

On the opposite page the Ballett des Landes Theaters, dancing in Fokine's Les Sylphides, *demonstrates pattern, while above, Lupe Serrano achieves the effect of flying.*

Below, from left to right, are examples of symmetry by Toni Lander and John Gilpin in Lander's Etudes *and of asymmetry by Nicholas Magallanes and Nora Kaye in Robbins'* The Cage.

Photos below: Baron Studios

Bertha Schaefer Gallery

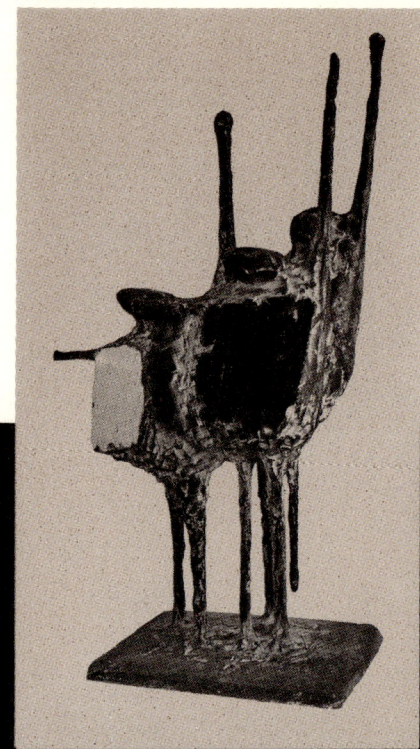

Left: two examples of dynamics in two different art forms: New Images of Man, *a sculpture by Peter Selz, and* Opus Jazz, *by Jerome Robbins.*

Right: Marlene Mesavage, dancing in Pan American, *uses distortion to increase the sense of flight.*

Dynamics is the expression, the varying strengths and gentleness of the stresses and force employed, the effort, the life energy.

Rolf Schafer

Martha Swope Photo/New York City Ballet

Distortion is the exaggeration or forcing of certain elements. Distortion always pulls the work away from an exact imitation and toward a particular point of view or emotion.

Any woman who paints her face or nails is practicing distortion, as is any, for that matter, who dyes her hair.

Animals do not use distortion. This is a human peculiarity; it is practiced for aesthetic and not for useful purposes.

In dancing, distortion is generally the stretching of tendons and joints beyond what is comfortable and easy. In religious dances, endurance becomes a kind of distortion. The very fact that a dancer has surmounted a real physical difficulty makes him extraordinary. His body is not like ours—it is special. He can do things we can't. This gives him power.

15

Stylization is the purposeful choice of unusual or distorted and unnatural means of expression.

But when distortion or virtuosity is practiced just for its own sake, because it is peculiar and hard to do, it ceases to be stylization, a purposeful exaggeration, and becomes merely stunting. Stunting and distorting are never dancing, and stringing together stunts is not choreography.

For instance, if we saw the two people in the paintings to the left walking down the street, we would know they were very, very ill. Purely from the standpoint of health, they are monsters.

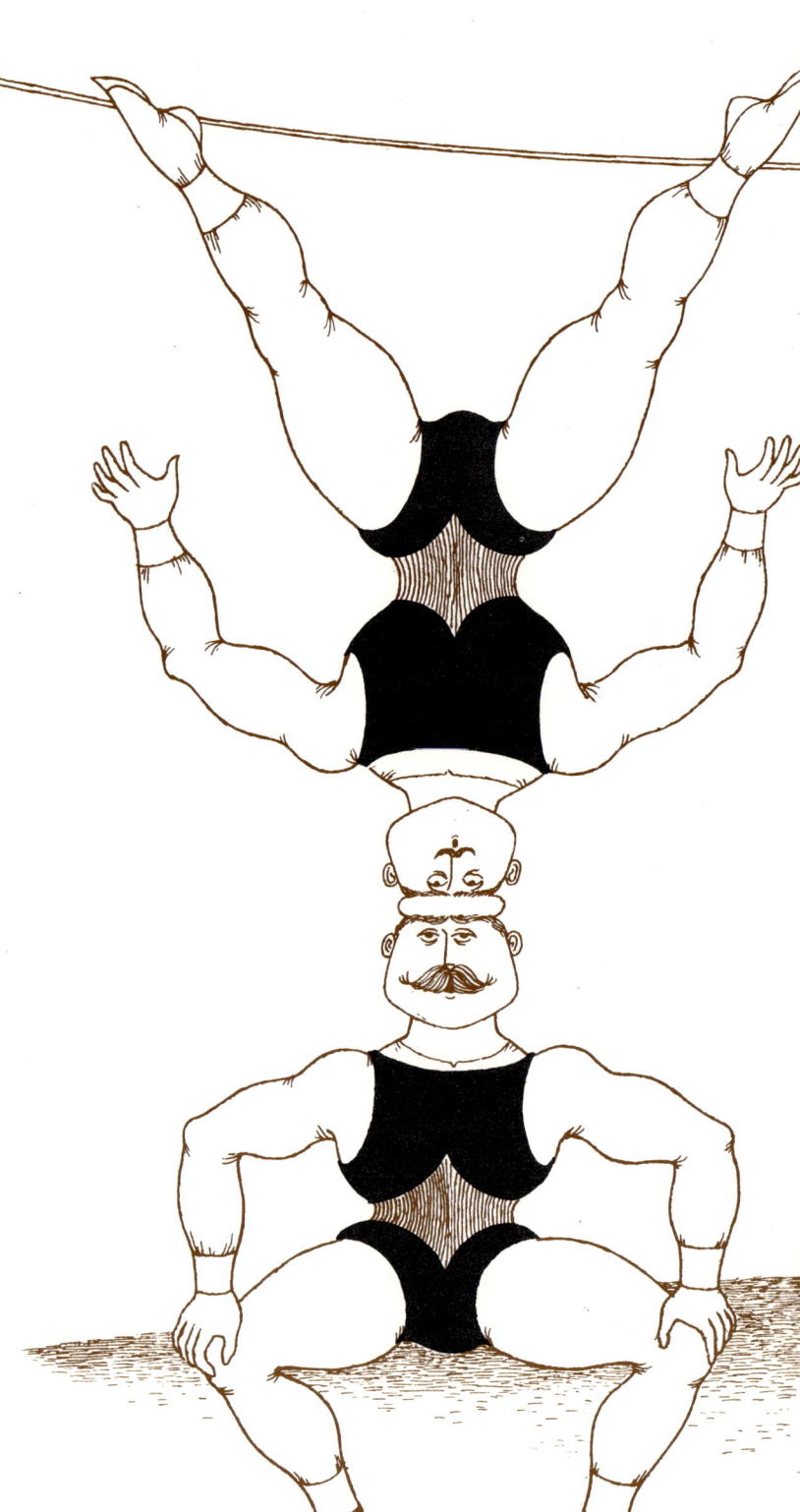

But in the painting, the attenuation and stretching of the man's neck and face express the burning fervor of his inner faith, his willingness to yield up his comfort to his vision. All the long lines suggest his denial of bodily ease, his using up of every part of his life in his yearning to reach God.

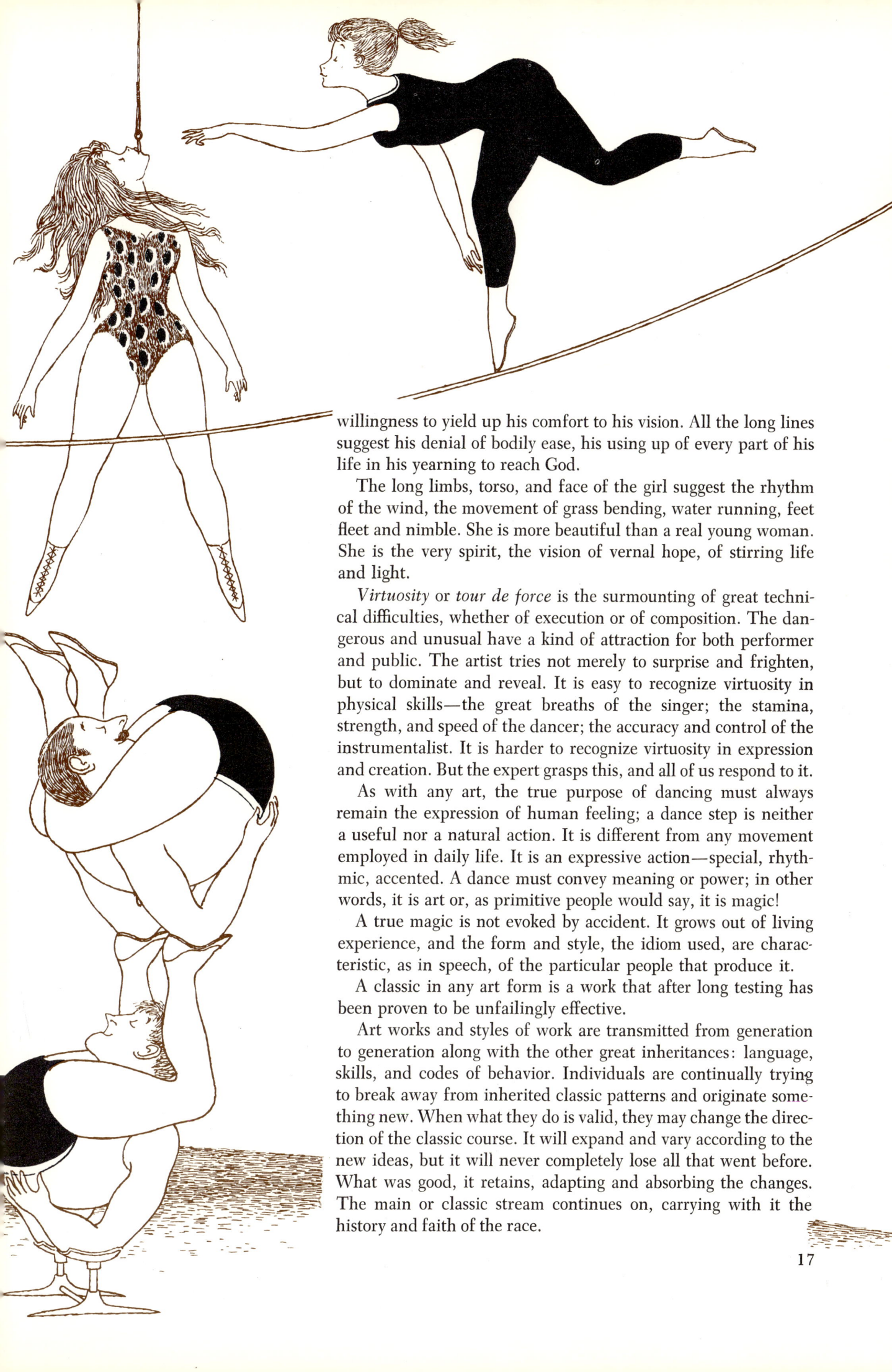

The long limbs, torso, and face of the girl suggest the rhythm of the wind, the movement of grass bending, water running, feet fleet and nimble. She is more beautiful than a real young woman. She is the very spirit, the vision of vernal hope, of stirring life and light.

Virtuosity or *tour de force* is the surmounting of great technical difficulties, whether of execution or of composition. The dangerous and unusual have a kind of attraction for both performer and public. The artist tries not merely to surprise and frighten, but to dominate and reveal. It is easy to recognize virtuosity in physical skills—the great breaths of the singer; the stamina, strength, and speed of the dancer; the accuracy and control of the instrumentalist. It is harder to recognize virtuosity in expression and creation. But the expert grasps this, and all of us respond to it.

As with any art, the true purpose of dancing must always remain the expression of human feeling; a dance step is neither a useful nor a natural action. It is different from any movement employed in daily life. It is an expressive action—special, rhythmic, accented. A dance must convey meaning or power; in other words, it is art or, as primitive people would say, it is magic!

A true magic is not evoked by accident. It grows out of living experience, and the form and style, the idiom used, are characteristic, as in speech, of the particular people that produce it.

A classic in any art form is a work that after long testing has been proven to be unfailingly effective.

Art works and styles of work are transmitted from generation to generation along with the other great inheritances: language, skills, and codes of behavior. Individuals are continually trying to break away from inherited classic patterns and originate something new. When what they do is valid, they may change the direction of the classic course. It will expand and vary according to the new ideas, but it will never completely lose all that went before. What was good, it retains, adapting and absorbing the changes. The main or classic stream continues on, carrying with it the history and faith of the race.

Delsartian rules for the positions of the hands

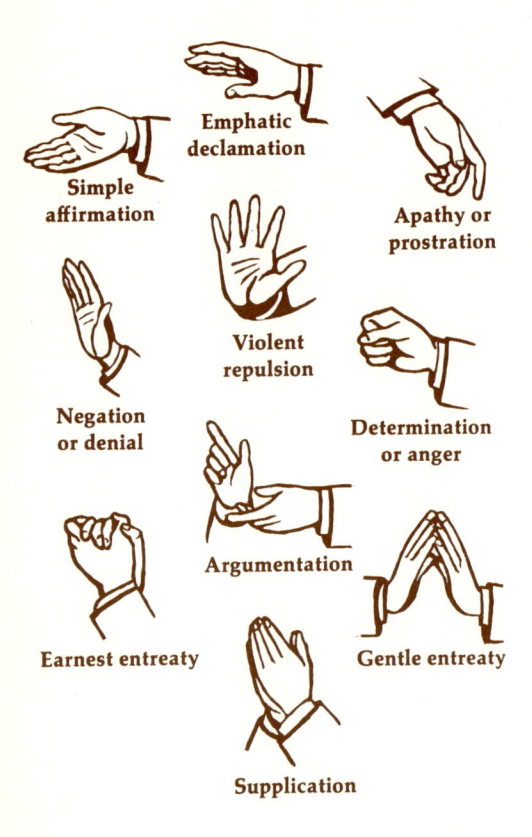

The Language of Dance

DANCE consists of three types of movement: instinctive actions and expressions, sign language, and dance steps.

Instinctive actions

On certain levels all men move alike. They walk alike, they run, crouch, and jump alike, they strike to kill, they cower in fear, they laugh, they sneer, they put out their hands in pity or love. These expressions of emotion, common to all men, are recognized by all. They are largely physiological. And many of man's basic movements are akin to animals'.

Dr. Martin Palmer at the Institute of Logopedics in Wichita, Kansas, has discovered that the most primitive forms of human movement are semi-swimming gestures closely resembling those made by amphibians, and that when the articulate and intellectual centers of control are destroyed in the brain, by disease or accident, these lower controls can be organized and taught. For example, a hand that has been helpless in spastic stricture from birth, that has even suffered muscular deterioration, when placed behind the back and rotated inward from the shoulder (as does a turtle's leg in swimming) can be made to open and shut voluntarily and taught to grasp and to handle tools and even, finally, to write.

Not only activities but expressions of emotion may be inherited from earlier stages of development. For instance, we show fear as all animals do. Our hackles rise, our hair bristles, our hearts pound, our lungs fill, we hold our breath to hear better, and brace our muscles for attack. Adrenalin pours through our bodies as it does through any beast's. In ordinary behavior the process is naturally not visible at full scale. But it needs only the slight widening of the pupil or nostril, the barest start or tensing, to give the sign. It has been suggested by Charles Darwin that at one point man could regurgitate at will and that now the turning aside of the head, the distending of nostril, the widening and lifting of lips to signify distaste are residues of this ability. The sneer is all that is left of the snarl; but the incisor tooth is still bared.

Everyone, even a little child, instantly recognizes dislike, anger, or fear. Love and kindness are also instantly recognized almost as though man had a sixth sense; but it is really the recognition of small signals.

Sign language

Beyond these instinctive, physical expressions, common to nearly all men in all times, there are learned, idiomatic gestures differing with cultural groups, and although similar and extending over many periods and territories, they are neither instinctive nor universal. Their relation to dancing lies in their prevalence and endurance.

Pantomime was resorted to when language was scant and inadequate. In time pantomime always tends to become formal and stylized.

Man through the ages has used stylized gesture for communication and expression.

Archives of the Staatliche Museen, Berlin-West

Albertina, Vienna

William Steinberg, Courtesy of Mr. and Mrs. Dario Soria

Sign language can be used to portray many things. Above: American Indians make the sign for "How many?" and the sign for "antelope"; and mourners from an Egyptian tomb indicate "Alas, we are bereft."

What do dances say? They say: "Take up thy bed and walk."

We find certain similar gestures in all parts of the world, such as nodding or shaking the head; extending the right hand in friendship, the weapon hand empty; uncovering the head as a mark of respect (originally this gesture was made with the head in the dust and the foot of the master on the neck). Many of the East Indian and Japanese dance gestures correspond to American Indian sign language. The Philippine Igorots use a thumbs-up movement in their victory dances that means life and survival to the warriors and puts one in mind of the "thumbs-up" signal for the sparing of life in the Roman arena centuries ago.

Each national group, however, as it develops its own spoken language, also develops certain deviations or idioms of the hands and face. Climate and custom shape these—as do degrees of civilization and native temperament.

Speaking of the development of the Greek language, Virginia Woolf wrote in *The Common Reader:* "With warmth, and sunshine, and months of brilliant, fine weather, life of course is instantly changed; it is transacted out of doors, with the result, known to all who visit Italy, that small incidents are debated in the street, not in the sitting-room, and become dramatic; make people voluble; inspire in them that sneering, laughing, nimbleness of wit and tongue peculiar to the Southern races, which has nothing in common with the slow reserve, the low half-tones, the brooding introspective melancholy of people accustomed to live more than half the year indoors."

Dance steps

Dance steps are peculiar to the tribe or people that evolves them, and in the case of creative artists, peculiar to the individual.

Dance steps are made up of expressive gestures common to all men, of pantomime and rhythmical exercises, which differ according to habits, to country and climate, to bodily characteristics, and, most particularly to the prevailing ideas of beauty.

When the purpose of dancing is serious—that is, part of living needs and not just for entertainment—it is often, but not always, the men of the community who do it.

Dances also say: "Give us this day our daily bread."

Laura Gilpin/Margretta S. Dietrich Collection

"Watch out!"

Photo Paul Popper

"Tra la la, hey, hey! and Cha-cha-cha!"

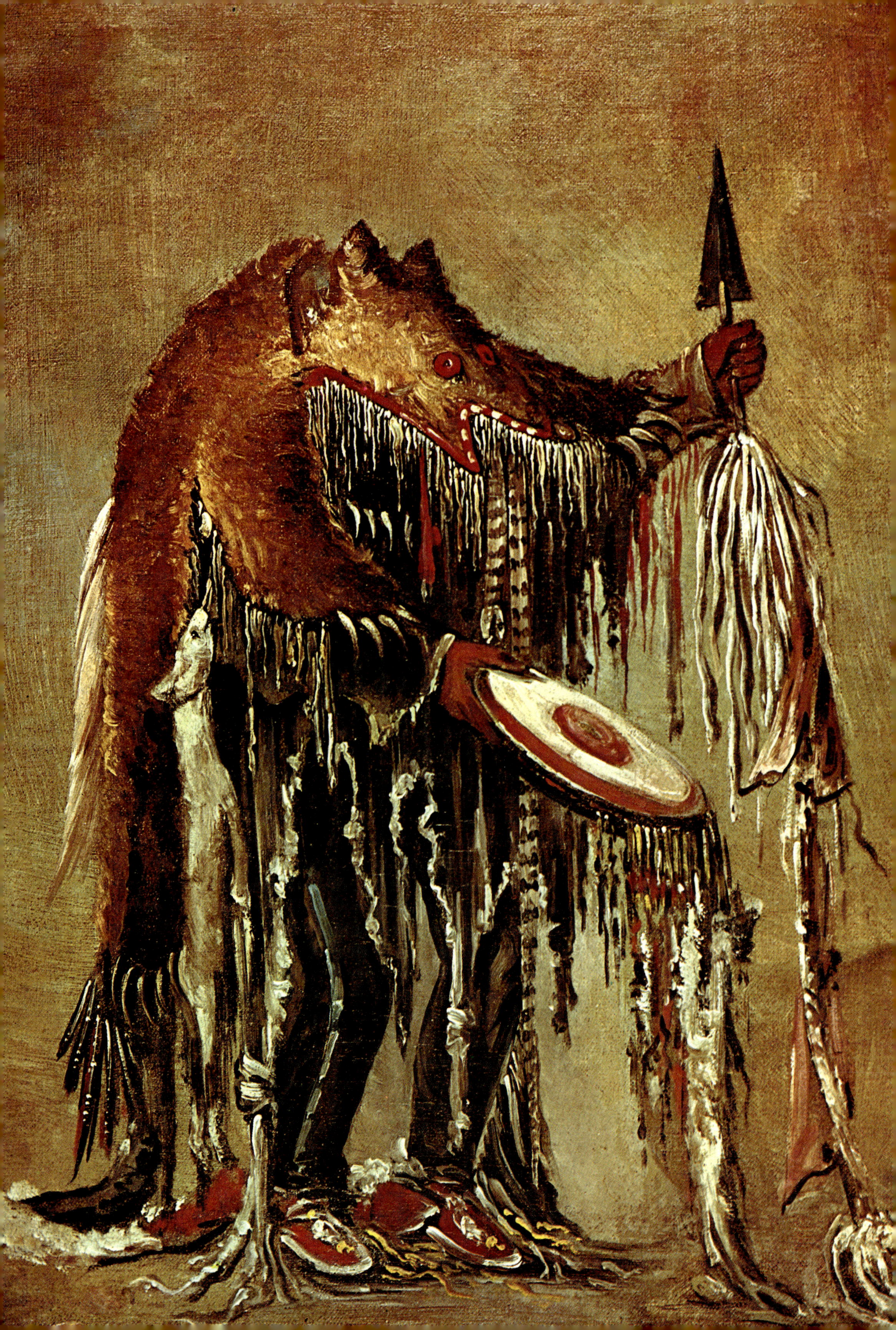

THERE is an element of religion or magic in all dances except those for entertainment.

Man knew his first religious experience in worshiping natural forces: thunder, rain, sun, moon, and animals. The animals of totems were thought not only to possess magic or godlike powers, but also to be closely related to particular individuals or tribes. In fact, the tribes took their identity from them, and long after men had ceased to worship animals, they carried the totem marks on their helmet crests and shields. The totem developed into an animal god—and later into a man God.

All primitives, like children, believe that if they act out something with the proper magic words, they can make it happen. This is called "sympathetic magic" or medicine.

The first dances nearly always involved imitation, and impersonation masks and ritualistic garments were employed. The dancer-priests first imitated desired events, then later acted out entire cycles in story fashion wearing masks which they believed either were the gods themselves or gave the wearer the power and terror of gods or ghosts. These commemorative services had power to change the lives of the participants and watchers as our religious services change ours. They were devised by and for illiterate people who could be reached only emotionally and whose instruction consisted of what they could be shown. All information, all moral training and ethics, all history were, of necessity, handed down in songs and dances, just as all race wisdom, the rules for health and conduct, the codes of behavior, the instruction in fighting techniques and crafts, find their way into mottos and jingles.

Strictly imitative gestures later gave place to formal symbolism and dancing, and with time were taken over by those people found to be the most effective in performance. These assisted the shamans, the medicine men or priests. These dances and gestures did not deviate from tradition. Any mistake or alteration would be displeasing to the gods.

The only religious dances we know today are performed by primitives and peoples of the Far East, who, such as our Amerindians whose dance chants are prayers, maintain in current practice their ancient rituals. The Christian church has no true religious dancing.

But other types of dances are performed around the world.

Dances for Health and Destruction

All peoples have prayers for health. Dances for health are called medicine dances, and nearly all primitives employ them. They obviously cannot be done by the central or star figure, who is generally in no condition to assist at the performance. Therefore, the ritual is carried out by a "medicine man" or priest, and consists of prescribed or recommended chants, the shaking or rattling of potent implements to scare away the devils that are plaguing the victim, and the general working up of sufficient rhythmic excitement to persuade the ill person that he is not so sick after all.

Blackfoot Medicine Man by George Catlin

Types of Dances

Medieval men believed that the plague was a punishment of the devil and could be driven from the body by mortifying the flesh. Vestigial exercises persist in the procession of flagellants at Seville and among the Penitentes of New Mexico.

In a Haitian voodoo rite, a woman walks over hot coals.

The interesting fact is that many times he does get well; perhaps he would not have without this encouragement.

Christ said, "Thy faith hath made thee whole"; this point of view lies behind all medicine dances.

Christians are not supposed to pray for destruction. But when it is done for reasons of competition, patriotism, or war, the practice is excused and even encouraged.

Until recently the British national anthem contained this second verse:

"O Lord our God arise,
Scatter our enemies,
And make them fall;
Confound their policies,
Frustrate their knavish tricks;
On Thee our hopes we fix;
God save us all."

It has been replaced by a stanza of opposite sentiment more in keeping with the desired international brotherly feeling.

The destructive dances, the dances for maiming or killing, belong to black magic—voodoo, the Jamaican Obeah, the Hawaiian Ana-Aná. These are based on hypnotic trance, the working up of great frenzies, praying against, not for, and they must always involve and center around some item of the victim's person or garments—old fingernail parings, a lock of hair, a torn fragment of dress, something personal that has been worn or used or touched. This detail may not be omitted.

The belief that power passes through direct touch, either of the person or of some part or belonging of the person, is universal and lies behind many religious services: the laying on of hands, for instance, in the ordaining of Christian priests; baptism; contact with any holy relic; and the curing of the king's evil (scrofula) by the king's touch on Maundy Thursday.

Children recognize the principle when they play "tag." The one "caught" must be actually touched—being seen is not enough.

Christians, being forbidden any religious dances, have none for either good or bad purposes.

Fertility Dances

Nearly all peoples have dances for rain, or the growing of crops, and for increase of animals and of children. These are called fertility dances and are often a form of sympathetic magic. A man gets on top of a house, for instance, and pours water down, or people walk about with green-growing branches. Sometimes a masked demon, who is a kind of clown, enters the village and chases the women and promises them children. This is the beginning of comedy, and there are many lusty jokes played during these ceremonies.

Fertility dances can be danced by the whole community or by specially chosen priests or leaders. Very often they are performed by men only.

In the agricultural stage of civilization, planting dances originated. As long as only women planted and men hunted, agriculture never entered ritual.

The Bacchanalia (performed in ancient Rome) were danced by men and women together. A bacchanal is a dance of worship of Bacchus, the God of nature's fertility cycle. Here the personal relation of the partners means nothing; they may never see each other again. They do not have to like each other; they are celebrating life.

There has always been a widespread craze for dancing after a great disaster, says James Laver. Following the Black Death, when three-quarters of Medieval Europe's population lay rotting or barely buried, and when a new generation was desperately needed to repopulate the stricken countries after the 30 Years' War, after the French Revolution, after the Napoleonic Wars, after World War I, dancing was universal and unrestrained in its quality. The whole population gave itself, unconsciously, of course, and quite spontaneously, to the current fertility rituals. They danced as though driven. And they danced without limiting decorums.

War and Hunting Dances

All war or hunting dances, whether old or current, are performed by men. The women, when permitted to attend at all, merely serve as a cheering section. (In certain tribes in Madagascar, West Africa, and North America, they are permitted to substitute for the men when the men are away fighting or hunting. The women not only keep the home fires burning, they war dance around them. This helps the men.) Nearly all primitive peoples have war dances to work up fighting excitement and courage.

Bettmann Archive

This is all that is left in our culture of the fertility ritual.

Mandan (American Plains Indians) buffalo dancers

A ritual dance of mourning from an Apulian tomb fresco in Ruvo.

All hunting or war dances employ sympathetic magic, that is, the acting out of the desired kill, with one warrior portraying the hunted animal or enemy, and others the triumphant victors. Indians have said that if they dance correctly, that is, if they have brought themselves into psychic sympathy with the animal, they then do not need to take great hunting precautions; the animal will allow itself to be killed. Part of the dancing is also propitiation, the begging pardon for the necessary death.

Most frequently war dances are done at the home base before taking off on a sortie, but occasionally they occur face to face with the enemy, and two great warriors will perform at each other in terrible mortal duet. This is the case in Java, and may have been in Greece. In Greece, because of the great scarcity of metal, representative champions were often entrusted with the decisive issue. Greek dances with weapons were called Pyrrichi. Socrates said: "The best dancer is also the best warrior." In the Middle Ages mass fighting was occasionally preceded by troubadours singing the merits of each side, while the war-horses pawed up the earth and the soldiers creaked and strained in their harness and balanced their huge iron spears and battle axes. The singing and pantomime gestures may have been excellent, but apparently they were never persuasive, because there is no record of both sides just applauding and going away.

At the end of a triumphant engagement, in every time and culture, there is always a tremendous spree at home for the benefit of the old men and the girls. Each event is acted out again and understatement is not the chief characteristic of the performance. The bags of scalps, heads, teeth, fingers, or weapons are used in rites concerning the soul-dismissal of the vanquished (that is, as an antidote against haunting), but the victors take an understandable pride, as well as a sense of importance, in the number and rank of the trophies. When the party is over, the prizes are used as costume or house decoration.

It does not matter what the technique; all war dances are performed for the purpose of displaying strength and summoning courage. The French Revolutionary Carmagnole raging through the streets of Paris after a good day with the guillotine was just such a dance of triumph. The citizens smeared their faces with the blood of the victims and dressed up in grizzly relics and tokens.

Our men do not present the scalps or heads of the enemy to their sweethearts, but they do bring back helmets, guns, decorations, bayonets, watches, and wedding rings. And there is here no thought of soul-dismissal—just the acquiring of mementos for the purpose of boasting. Their dances are improvised, however, without ceremony and are performed after the ordeal to let off steam. It might be a good idea if our soldiers danced before battle—it would help their nerves.

Dances for Death and Rebirth

There are dances for births and dances for rebirths or death. Dances at deaths and funerals have been common in all times. This is because dancing was formerly not considered a mere outpouring of jolly spirits but magic ritual, and by putting in direct

The Royal Watusi spear dancers of Rwanda, Africa

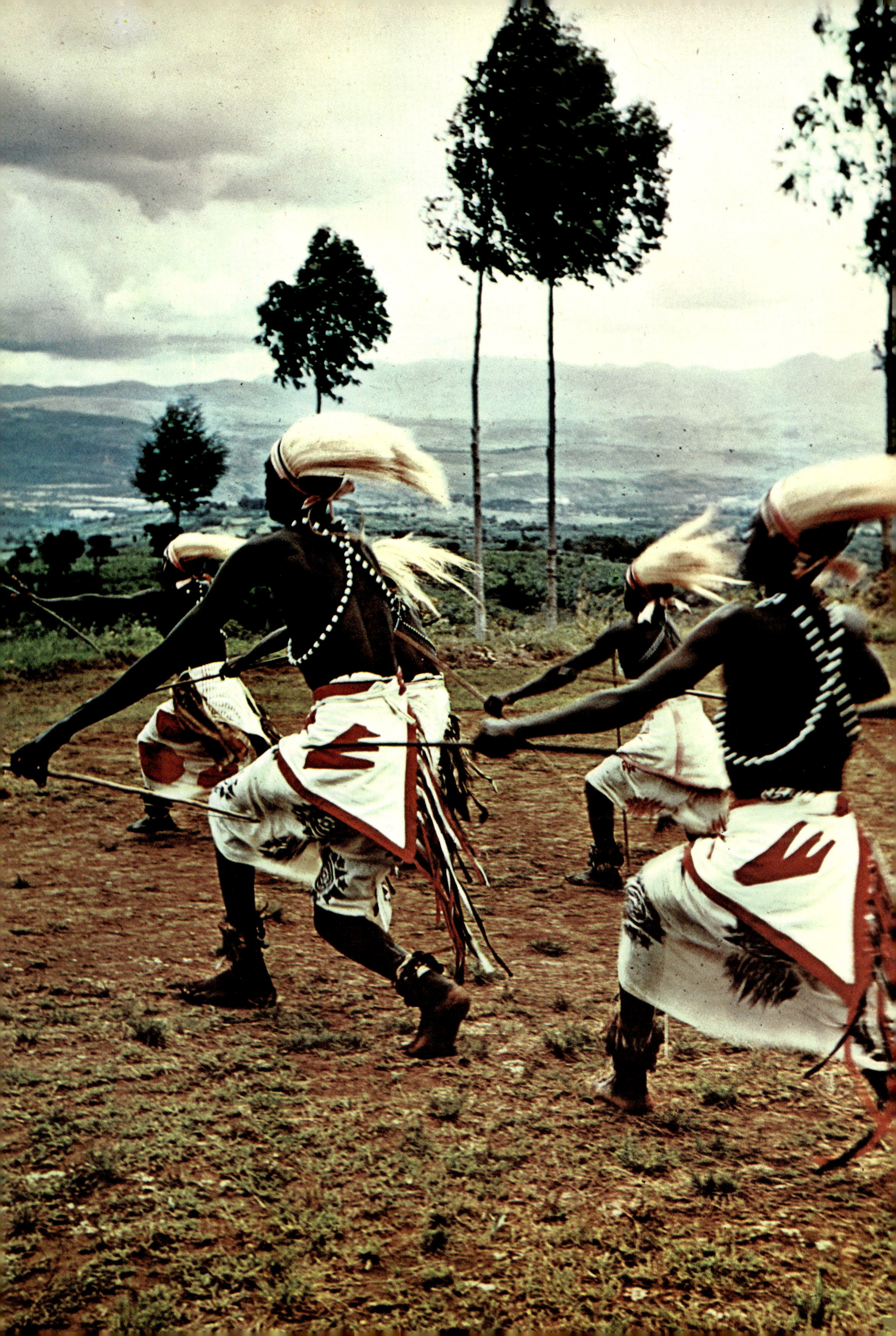

In an etching by Doré, a 19th-century Andalusian Danse Funèbre *is performed about the bier.*

Two primitive Australians perform a totemistic dance.

contrast the most vital expression of life, the moving body, and lifeless clay, the celebrants thought to guarantee for the deceased a rebirth and spell out resurrection for him. The dances were sometimes to comfort the dead, sometimes to remind him of duties or to ward off evil spirits, but in all cases there was a reaffirmation of continuing life, and the exercise was probably good for the mourning kinsmen because it forced them to release their grief in physical exertion.

Certain American Indian tribes danced whenever a death occurred. The Philippine Igorots dance around a dead warrior from dawn until noon, shouting to him to wake up. They shake him to help him. In New Ireland mourning dances are done annually in one jumbo village celebration during the month of June. A new corpse is not always available; happily it is not required. Special funeral dresses and hair-dos are worn and dancers in handsome masks appear in place of the dead and are recognized, called by name, and saluted with wild lamentations by everyone.

The Ju-Ju of West Africa is not only a solemn ceremony of raising dead ghosts but, like many spiritualistic practices, highly commercial. The spirits are generally materialized in the form of their own particular animal totem. The totem mask is worn by a dancer expert in terrifying.

In Australia the natives believed that no man could die naturally. It followed that the deceased was killed either by a man or a spirit. The dance by the family trying to determine the responsible murderer, for purposes of revenge or propitiation, was therefore sometimes complicated.

Secular funeral dances, until recently, were not restricted to savages; all of antiquity employed them. Pavanes (a slow medieval dance) were performed at many a lying-in-state in Spain. Funeral jotas are still used in Valencia. Until 1840 in Bailleul in northern France, young maidens danced in the very nave of their church around the bier of a companion, and in Scotland, until the 19th century, it was accepted practice for a widow to leap in a lively strathspey beside her husband's corpse, and it was a mark of small affection if she could not bring herself to do it with some enthusiasm.

Many dances of death and rebirth are incorporated into the initiation ceremonies at which a primitive youth enters manhood; he must pass tests of bravery and submit to a ritualistic death and rebirth before he is admitted as a fully qualified warrior to his tribe. The youths learn that the masked gods who have terrified them were not supernatural at all, but companions and fellow tribesmen. They promise never to tell the women and children.

Peace Dances

Tribes in New Ireland who have been fighting all year meet on May 1 (a date seemingly significant for all peoples) and dance and feast together harmoniously and happily until sundown. Then something—it can be anything—is made to happen that will serve as an excuse for another twelve months of bloodshed. One would suppose that few acquaintances survived more than two or three of these ominous reunions.

Play Dances

Play dances began with animal worship—imitative jokes and games. When man stopped believing in his totem gods, he kept the dances because they were fun to do.

Dances for play and singing games are generally performed by children. The same dances, when performed by adults, become courtship dances.

There are some dances, however, that adults do simply to cheer themselves up. These dances are mainly for men, who play more easily than women. In our civilization men have always had more leisure. Women seem never to have been able to get children and cooking off their minds enough to have fun among themselves.

The hornpipe was not originally a sailor's dance but a solo jig done to bagpipes. Because it was a solo, men without partners could do it anywhere. British sailors for hundreds of years have danced it whenever they have felt gay and excited; on shore in anticipation of a great voyage, or on a rolling deck at sea to remind themselves that there was land and that this land was home.

There are many similar dances done by peasants—French, Tyrolean, Basque, Russian, Yugoslav, solo performances by men and for men just as an expression of high spirits and camaraderie. In some southern European countries the men dance together in the wine shops after church on Sundays. The steps to these friskings are frequently improvised. They often, as might be expected, include horse-play and rough-and-tumble, wrestling and hitting. They are done purely for fun, because they feel satisfying.

The snake dances connected with football games, the exuberant horseplay on carrier flight decks and in barracks at times of particular tension are all examples of play dances as a release of pent-up emotion.

Besides these improvisations, there are proper dance games, enactments of historic episodes, when the villagers express their feelings in improvised community performances. These dances demonstrate concern over particular happenings, rather than universal and recurring situations as birth and death, fertility, war, or marriage. They are, in fact, the beginning of western theater, and the germ out of which eventually developed opera and story-ballet (*ballet d'action*).

Most children's games are just such old rituals adapted and simplified—maypole dances, musical chairs, ring-around-a-rosy, blind man's buff (also used in courtship), tossing the dummy. They also include ancient singing games like:

"Have you any bread and wine.
For we are the Romans."
"No, we have no bread and wine,
For we are the English soldiers."
-or-
"Sur le pont d'Avignon
L'on y danse, l'on y danse."
-or-
"Who killed cock-robin?"

Many of the death and resurrection dances of heathen Europe have become play dances.

Werner/Austrian State Tourist Dept.

This schuhplattler, performed by the Heimatgruppe Goldegg in Salzburg, was originally a virile play dance including hitting and slapping.

To express their joy at a royal visit by Victoria to the British flotilla at Plymouth in 1846, the sailors give vent to their delight in a hornpipe.

Culver Pictures, Inc.

Mt. Hagen Maiden, East Central New Guinea

Some courtship preparations are more demanding than others.

Courtship Dances

Courtship dances are always done by those special people interested and not by substitutes or priests. No matter what the style, they all serve the same purpose: to introduce boys and girls who wish to get married. They often involve kissing and trials of strength, or any kind of game that will get people on a friendly footing or show off their best points.

"This courtship has the virtue of attracting hearts to one another and inducing love.... Dancing is practiced to make manifest whether lovers are in good health and sound in all their limbs, after which is permitted to them to kiss their mistresses whereby they may perceive if either has an unpleasant breath or exhales a disagreeable odor as that of bad meat so that in addition to divers other merits attendant on dancing, it has become essential to the well-being of society."—says Monk Arbeau in his book, *Orchésographie,* written in 1588.

In all communities where the dances are part of real courtship, they are courteous, gallant, charming, and pleasant. The more primitive the people, the more restrained the gesture. Sometimes, as in Samoa, the responses are made only with the eyes. When the dances become rough or vulgar, they reflect a disintegration in the community life.

Our square dances are courtship dances and so are all our ballroom or social dances. The meaning is perfectly plain and never varies: boy meets girl.

Entertainment or Theater

The art dance or theater, which includes the ballets of all nations, is the one dance form that has no magic significance for the performers, because it is removed from life.

Performance ceases to be ritual and becomes theater when the actor no longer performs for his own purpose and satisfaction, but purely as proxy or substitute on behalf of the audience.

Theater came from the rain-making magics and the celebrations of the earth's fertility and rebirth through the resurrection of a god. Gradually the gestures grew formal until the original drama was barely indicated. Gradually also the blood sacrifices were abandoned and token sacrifice substituted. At first, a king was killed each year as intermediary for his tribe or people. Later a chosen hero was substituted for the king. And still later, a criminal was substituted for the king or hero. This proved economic all around. It effected a great saving of kings, who were valuable; it got rid of undesirables; and it furnished spectacle.

"The towering terrors of superstition no longer hung over the mask," says Kenneth MacGowan, in *Masks and Demons,* "and as the terrible spirit of the demon goes out of the mask, the spirit of play which has always been in it increases."

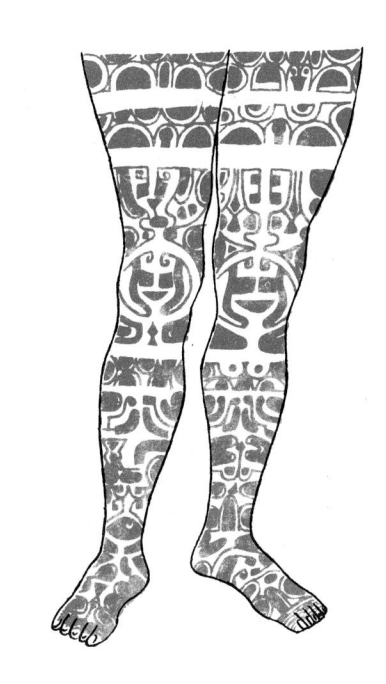

Below: the Cornish Furry dancers of today have forgotten that this dance originated to celebrate the riddance of an evil spirit.

British Travel Association

Museum of the American Indian

The Development of Western Dance

DANCING has a history as old as the race of man, but most ancient dancing has been lost because there was no way of recording movement. Long, long after speech was written or pictured, men found an exact way to notate musical sound. But it was only in this century that a means (motion pictures) was found to record dance performances and only in this decade that methods of notating dance movement were perfected.

Unhappily, most of the older styles, and all old individual works are gone—all the dances of antiquity (together with all antique music), all the dances of the Middle Ages, and most of the dances of the Renaissance and the so-called Pre-Classic period (1550-1680). Individual pieces have survived only where a school, a formal religious tradition (as in the Orient), or an enduring theater has furnished the means of preserving works and their way of being performed.

However, we can reconstruct approximately the history of dancing. In Africa, in the South Pacific, in Central and South America, and in the southwestern United States there are primitive dances being performed that probably do not vary greatly from those done a thousand years before. There are ritual and religious dances in the Orient that have endured as long. There are theatrical forms in China, Java, and Japan that are at least 800 years old. There are European folk dances that reflect, in greatly modified form, antique celebrations. And there are scriptures, pictures, bas-reliefs (none of them in movement of course, and therefore with no indication of rhythm) from which we can deduce something. We can use our wits and guess.

For instance, we can guess how men danced from the way they fought and the weapons they used; from the clothes they wore and the musical instruments they played; from their customs and their manners; from the relation between men and women and that between men and their rulers. And we can guess much from the traditional inherited dances that exist today.

The surest clue as to the accuracy of our guesses is to dance out the steps. If they dance well, we have probably guessed correctly—no people ever bothered to do what was dull or ineffective.

Prehistoric dancing

All primitives, all people who go barefoot and hunt unprotected by armor, have certain characteristics in common. They stamp out rhythms. They run crouched low in imitation of animals or of the precautionary attitudes adopted when stalking prey or an enemy. The primitive feels himself akin to the animals as no civilized man ever does because the primitive man lives closer to the animals, with greater direct dependence on them and peril from them.

He has to face his enemy or his prey naked. He is vulnerable, and so he bends to the ground to protect his vitals and for magic power. Whatever the posture, crouching over the earth or yearning toward the sky, he is seeking help. He has great need of help. He must pacify or cope with forces that he feels will destroy him sooner or later.

His feet are like an animal's; they trust and know the earth. He uses his feet with a sensitivity and response impossible to the man who wears shoes. The primitive hand is still a fist; it clutches; it strikes and pounds.

He stresses rhythm rather than body line or posture. He uses his arms not for balance or design, but in imitative mime or rhythmic accents. He sings or emits cries to encourage himself and to frighten his enemies. The body and foot rhythms are complex, as with all people who communicate by drums and who use rhythm as stimulation. The visual patterns tend to be simple; performing skill or muscular virtuosity counts for almost nothing. Endurance, belief, intensity, and exact attention to rules are what matter and what make the magic work. Even as with us, faith counts in prayer far more than a fine voice.

The primitive wears ritual and magic talismans. All markings and decorations are purposeful and traditional and never chosen at personal whim. He always paints his face or he wears a mask.

The similarities of primitive dancing may be seen in the New Stone Age drawing from the Hoggar Mountains of North Africa above and the American Indians below.

In all cultures from earliest times men have worn masks. At first, these masks symbolized the god or the animal imitated or invoked. The dancer became the god—quite literally. Later, by putting on the mask, he only assumed god-like or magic powers. The mask with its aura of magic was itself powerful, as in our civilization the cross or the national flag is believed to be. We still use ritualistic garments in our own religious services. No priest performs any serious office without first putting on his stole. And just as a priest puts on ceremonial copes to invest himself with power, or a king his crown and orb, a French senator his sash of office, the primitive dancer in ritual wears a mask. It gives permission, and it gives power. It obliterates personal identity, responsibility, and limitation. The wearer is no longer just himself.

Primitives rarely touch their partners or dancing companions. Men and women seldom dance together, except in the most rigid ritualistic pattern (or at other times in abandoned frenzies of permitted communal orgy). Usually they dance in separate groups, the men in their special dances and the women in theirs.

We may suppose that prehistoric man followed these rules. What their rhythms or patterns were we do not know. The basic forms undoubtedly developed: the ring, which is always magic, with everyone equal and one part as strong and as prominent as another; the arch, which suggests birth; the straight line, which rarely occurs in nature and is therefore exciting; and unison movement, which never occurs in nature and is therefore extraordinary.

Most primitive dances go on for many hours at a stretch, long enough for the performer to get thoroughly worked up. His heart beat adjusts to match the beat of the drum, his breath quickens and brings to his lungs and brain heady draughts of oxygen. He grows into a state of steadily mounting excitation with a developing sense of power and endurance.

In certain primitive dances, notably those in Africa and Malaya, repeated whirling and spinning, or the rapid raising and lowering of the head induces a state of dizziness and trance, a true bewitchment in which ordinarily painful or dangerous experiences can be surmounted with ease. Under these conditions Asians, East Indians, and Africans can walk over beds of hot coals apparently without their feet being burned, stab themselves, or lift inert hypnotized children on the points of spears without breaking their skin. The Burmese pierce themselves with knives and steel pins without drawing blood. In this state of exaltation the American Indians submitted to terrible physical tortures, sometimes including the cutting off of fingers or toes. Even today, the Hopis carry live rattlesnakes in their teeth without being bitten. These rattlers are complete with venom sacs and have not been domesticated.

In ancient and primitive ceremonials, the dancers often went further; animals and human beings were sacrificed.

All men seal important actions in blood. The spilling of blood makes the magic effective; it is the price. Pirate documents were signed in blood. A child's promise is "Cross my heart and hope to die." At one point someone always did die to make the promise stick.

Preparation for the hunt, Masai dance, Africa

Photo Paul Popper

On the whole, primitive dances, unless they involve a killing of some sort, have no dramatic pattern and seem to move along without climax. The dancers dance until they have had enough to satisfy their needs. Then they stop. They are not dancing to make an effect on an audience, and there is no applause. In some dances the rhythm quickens with the excitement; in many it does not. In most Amerindian dances it maintains a steady beat without pause for ninety minutes or more. The ceremonies go on for days.

Nearly all of these dances are ritualistic, with special rules and requirements. Free improvisation is not encouraged except as an aftermath. For instance, in the southwestern Rain or Corn Dances, when the rains actually begin to fall, the men hurl themselves on the ground and roll in the mud, and universally after any victory in war or election most restraints are off.

We must not despise these primitive dances as childish. They are performed with more belief and sincerity than any dances we ourselves do. Also, when the Indians dance, the rains do actually come. Never forget that. Of course, they take care to perform them during the rainy season.

Early Mediterranean Civilizations

All cultures and civilizations influence us to some degree, but the five that most directly shaped our way of living in Western Europe and America were the five great early Mediterranean civilizations of the Bronze and Iron Ages: the Egyptian, Hebrew, Greek, Roman, and Mesopotamian. The ancient civilizations of the East played no part in our formation. Alexander conquered India in the 4th century B.C. and later a certain amount of commercial traffic was conducted under the Romans. But the exchange was restricted mainly to material objects and did not involve arts, religion, or culture. Not until the Crusades and the subsequent opening of trade routes (1200-1400) did ideas from the Orient, from China, India, Persia, and the Spice Islands, begin to reach us consistently. Our ways of thinking by then had been fairly set. We had become a civilization with our own characteristics and our own basic point of view.

The warrior is now better armed than the primitive. His head and torso are protected by metal. His shield is made of metal, no longer of animal hide or wood, and he now holds death off at the end of a bronze or iron sword. His arrows are metal-tipped, not stone, shell, or bone. He has catapults and battering rams and other elaborate machines for waging war. He recognizes and obeys codes of fighting and dying that are not simple taboos based on magic and fear, but rules of ethics and honor.

He fights upright and with wide gestures. His armor permits him to do this and his pride and honor demand it. Under his helmet he holds his head high. He no longer tattoos his face with magic marks, but before doing anything important, particularly before going into battle, he prays and makes sacrifices. He believes fervently in omens. He believes in fate; this makes him less fearful. In his dancing, as in all ways of life, he moves with a new nobility and freedom.

Michel Huet/Multiphoto

Ivory Coast dancers with hypnotized child

Hopi snake dance

Photo Paul Popper

Early Etruscan dancing girl (Courtesy Museum of Fine Arts, Boston)

He opens his hands. Those people who think in terms of loving human relations, who are interested in the arts of peace and philosophy, rather than just in fighting one another, open their fists and fingers. The hand of the Bronze Age Man is now no longer a weapon; it is something to take hold of, to give and communicate with; it is an extension of the language—it is a voice. The palm is used to sculpt the air. Many love dances brush the air and the direction of the partner with the exposed palm; no war-dance would contain these movements. It is only in moments of deep emotion that adults use their palms to caress or slap; they use their fingers when they begin to exchange ideas.

The Iron Age man is both horseman and athlete. A man with a horse can conquer space and speed, freed in part from the pull of the ground. He is not a slave of the earth like the barefoot savage. You can tell this by his feet. He stamps on the ground. He glides over it. He lifts off it. He leaps. He is the master.

The Bronze Age man is aware of beauty, not only as magic but as a quality in itself. This is a great step forward. He brings his crafts, buildings, and sculpture to a high level. Beauty of line is a vital factor in his life; posture and gestures are valued for appearance as well as for meaning. Visual patterns are devised because their form gives pleasure—a step beyond mere rhythm patterns. Dances become a sequence of movement in which over-all design plays a leading part.

Etruscan tomb of the Triclinium, c. 470 B.C.

Alinari/Art Reference Bureau

Egyptian dancing girls, tomb painting, Thebes, c.1950 B.C.

This is an *Egyptian*. His civilization lasted four thousand years. To him we owe geometry, complex weaving, paper, the concept of rewards and punishments after death, and, most notably, the exact recording of history. His sculpture and his architecture, although flowering more than four thousand years ago, rank in line and execution with any since.

And they last. We owe him, therefore, the example of attempting the impossible, the defiance of death. He tried to make cloth, buildings, and even dead bodies immortal. And he nearly succeeded. He wished things, the things he made and the things he used, to last forever. This was a new idea in the world and so contrary to human experience as to be attractive long after his civilization had perished. His government and his religion are known even if they have no influence; his language we read with understanding and theories as to its pronunciation.

His longing for life after death, for immortality, is still with us. Today, thousands of years after he passed from the world, the flowers buried in his tombs retain their color. His linen and jewels lie folded around the flesh of his kings, still recognizable.

How did he dance? We can only guess. His music is totally lost. We know from the bas-reliefs that dancing was important to him and used on all occasions, particularly in religious services.

The Egyptians liked acrobatics and athletics, and used copper cymbals, tambourines, bone clackers, castanets, drums, and pipes. They danced to orchestras of lyres and choral chanting. We may suppose that the same qualities characterized their dances that characterized their other art forms, which were restrained and formal and of fine pattern.

Because of the stylized convention in all Egyptian reliefs, it is hard to know if the dancers really turned their hands and feet sideways and stiffened their fingers, or whether, as is more likely, this

Pharaoh Mycerinus and his queen, Fourth Dynasty

Egyptian dancer and acrobat, c.1180 B.C.

was simply a pictorial convention. It is hard to believe people would do anything so dull as shift from one flat position to another.

The Asians learned early to use the hand with open fingers; the Egyptians may have been among the first. The hands on the Egyptian reliefs are important and eloquent, although the hands of the statues are frequently shown in absolute repose.

No Egyptian lounges or sprawls or stands on uneven weight or lifts a hip. These men and women move with purpose, or they wait and watch with majesty. They may have in their later periods (c. 1500 B.C.), after Oriental influence made itself felt, rippled the spine and hips in the Oriental manner. The people living around the Nile now do.

Under the Egyptian, there began to appear trained dancers, professional entertainers, owned and maintained by the courts, and special priests, priestesses, and celebrants. These functioned like the choir in a church. Possibly the first soloists made their entry at this time—a solo dance has been documented as early as 2400 B.C. and professional dancers are in representations of the 4th millenium. We do not have any similar people in our civilization today. These were for the most part people of lower class, that is, male slaves and all women except princesses.

William H. Greene/Photo Researchers

Above: Israeli harvest festival dance.
Below: Margalith Oved, leading Inbal (Folk Ballet) dancer

This is a *Hebrew* whom the Egyptians held in bondage for five hundred years and used as slave labor to build their cities and tombs. To the Hebrew we owe our religion, our concept of one God, who is our Father. The Egyptian king, Akhenaton (1358 B.C.), preached solar-monotheism, but his teachings were overruled by his priests and did not last. The Hebrew's God is also the Christian God. The Hebrew gave us moral law, prophetic vision, and the legends and songs by which we instruct ourselves and approach all mysteries. He established forever the fact that man cannot be destroyed through cruelty or oppression, but only by moral weakness and sin. He placed in the scale of human experience suffering as a seal on inner virtue, as the fixative for high purpose. He gave us the sublime example of hope and pride enduring. Of all the peoples of the ancient world, he alone survived because he had a stout heart and disciplined himself — and because he never, at any moment in time, then or since, lost hope.

It has been thought that the great religious influence of the Hebrews over the surrounding civilizations was that their God was unseen, without picture or statue, and therefore limited or defined in no way. This unseen God could be all things to all men.

All other antique cultures changed or disappeared. The Hebrew or Israelite alone has maintained the definitive characteristics of his moral and religious ways of living, uninfluenced and unpolluted by any of the many cultures among which he has lived. The point of view that served him at the time of pyramid building serves him just as well today. We have here a survival of antiquity more potent than the entombed Egyptian flowers and grain.

Israel Government Tourist Office

Shepherd dance, Inbal

Israel Government Tourist Office

Margalith Oved and Dahlia Kubani

Israel Government Tourist Office

But Hebrew music and dancing, together with all their other arts, are gone. In common with all Levantine peoples, Israel was conquered again and again. Her tribes were scattered, her wealth was destroyed, and her cities were violated. The immigrant Hebrews absorbed the customs of their new neighbors except where these impinged on their religious beliefs and moral code. In these areas they rejected all influence, and established a resistance to change unique among contemporary religions. Their arts, however, were not so cherished and shortly were nearly unidentifiable.

The music of their present traditional ritual is very old but not ancient, not the music of Moses or David. It is probably not more than 1,200 to 1,400 years old, and of either Slavic or Spanish origin. This is true also of the dances which have been exposed for hundreds of years to Arab and Slavic influences.

In ancient Israel it is unlikely that men and women danced together freely—the women were kept in subjugation. No woman danced outside her home. When Salome danced, it was for one man, the king, and she was considered out of order in many ways.

Even today among the Yemenite Jews, men and women dance separately in separate rooms, even at bridal festivals. The groom does not see his chosen one, nor touch her hand, until after the ceremony is completed and he takes her to his home.

These dances are all restricted in movement, as might be expected from a people who have lived largely shut away in ghettos. The steps are shuffling, confined to the ground; the arms are held close to the sides or clasped close on neighbors' shoulders; the hands are closed (for all gestures, even conversational ones), and the fingers are held in a bunch with the thumb and little finger touching. It is a hand that seeks not to expose itself. It is secretive, a small weapon.

These dances and dance habits are obviously old—how old we cannot be sure. It is doubtful that these confined patterns applied to the free tribes of ancient Israel.

The dances now performed in Israel are adaptations of foreign forms. Modern Israel is a new country with new ideals. The men and women stand at last on equal footing, and they dance equally, with free-swinging steps and runs (very unlike the Arabic or Oriental sources) and free and beautiful use of the arms. This is new and quite deliberate. A great many of the new citizens came from Western Europe and they brought their Western point of view with them. The Israeli people are evolving a dance suitable to their present culture and their present way of life. It reflects little of the ancient manners and forms.

But the ancients held dancing in great esteem. In the Psalms every kind of musical instrument is mentioned. David, you will remember, danced before the Ark of the Lord, and all high festivals and rejoicings were marked with religious dancing.

"Is not this David the king of the land? did they
not sing one to another of him in dances?"
I SAMUEL XXI: 11

"And David danced before the Lord with all his might."
II SAMUEL VI: 14

Hermes with the Infant Dionysus
by Praxiteles

This is a *Greek* of the Golden, or Periclean, Age. He gave us our philosophy, logic, mathematics, medicine. He gave us our concept of man as not merely a member of a tribe or a religious group, as not the subject of a king, but as a citizen—a free inhabitant of a city. He gave us above all the idea of art as a necessary factor in daily life. And he left us examples to justify and prove this claim. His sculpture, architecture, poetry, and drama have become the great touchstones for the Western World since.

All we know of him, everything he left, is valuable. And so we must grieve that his music and dance have perished. Only faint indications of ancient Greek music remain in folk songs and in the rituals of the Orthodox Church. The creations of ancient Greek choreographers are gone, and the pictures of dancing in the reliefs and vase paintings only tantalize us.

But we do know that the Greeks practiced all kinds of physical discipline. They were great athletes. They danced mostly naked, hence they must have employed vigorous movement. We see that they liked free running and skipping and jumping, always with harmony of line and wide scope of expression, and in easy open postures without any apparent artificiality. There appears to be no acrobatic distortion of any kind.

Girls and boys, youths and maidens, danced freely together. Except in ritualistic orgies honoring Aphrodite and Dionysus, men and women danced separately.

Many of the reliefs show considerable humor, and there is a recurring element of mockery and play.

The role of the fool, the clown, the satyr, the koshari (Amerindian) has had mystic importance right down to the present day. They are the men who dare what for others would be impious or disrespectful, these are the middlemen, the liaison figures between human law and divine power. These people commune with the underground, speak to the dead, mock the king, and by doing so hearten the common man. No society has ever tried to live without them. They have different names in different cultures. They are always the same person, the voice of truth, the critic, the only possible approach to the Gods.

Like the primitives before them, the ancients believed in the magic power of dancing. In many ways the Greeks still lived on a primitive level, believed in the magic power of dancing, and indulged in drunkenness and sacrifice during the ceremonials. These were pleasing to the gods and therefore good for the community. Nearly everything the ancients did while dancing was pleasing to the gods. What people do together with the sanction of their laws is very different in its effect on the performer from what an individual does alone in defiance of law or custom. The Dionysian orgies, for all their excesses, were not at all like our drunken parties. There were rules, there was a purpose, and the people felt no guilt afterwards. The Greeks believed gay celebrations were an important part of their spiritual life, and wild behavior was not condemned.

In these dances they used ritualistic and symbolic costumes and masks, sometimes for magic or religious purposes, sometimes for mischief. Much was forgiven a masker. What, for instance, might

Pierre M. Martinot
Olympia Museum

have been considered an impertinence on the part of the butcher or one's husband's business partner was considered pretty good fun from a costumed satyr.

There have always been times when masks make naughty actions permissible, as during Halloween or Mardi Gras. On the other hand there are times when they do not, as in highway robberies. It all depends on whether the community has joined in the game. Most of these celebrations occurred at the same seasons ours do and for the same reason: for the death of the old king or god, the birth of the new.

With the ancient Greeks, dancing assumed a place in civilization it has not held since. One of the seven Muses, on an equal plane with the muses of epic poetry and music, was Terpsichore, the Muse of Dancing.

Maenad in Dionysiac dance

Greek youth and dancing girl with castanets

Greek leap dancers

This is a *Roman*. His was the largest empire in the ancient world. Men trembled at his name from Spain to India, and from the Scottish Highlands to the Upper Nile. He gave us law, language, our alphabet, our calendar, roads, government by tribune, the organization of states into a central government. The round keystone arch, aqueducts, rules for managing armies and battles, as well as workable schemes for subjugating whole nations and making them foot the bill. He left us no enduring religion, and little philosophy, but some astonishing architecture and fine epic verse, love lyrics, oratory, and reporting.

The educated Romans looked on Greece as the mother of culture and all civilized refinements, just as the 18th-century Americans looked on England and all European and Slavic countries looked on France. The elite of Rome spoke Greek and aped her arts and literature. As with most imitations, the vitality faded.

Although Rome's original arts, painting, mosaic work, engineering, lyric and epistolary writing, were strong, its later sculpture and architecture cannot compare with the best Greek works. The Roman drama and, we presume, music and dancing were likewise inferior. The Romans, at first, like the Greeks, had stressed beauty, notably in the use of the hand, of which Seneca says:

"We admire the dancers because their hands can describe all things and all sentiments, and because their expressive gestures are as quick as words. Every change of the position of the hands and of the individual fingers expresses a different meaning."

This subtle use of the hand was soon lost to the West. Dance gestures became brutalized and vulgar.

What had been restrained and harmonious in Greece changed in later Rome to what was sensational and violent. Blood sacrifice had previously been used purely for punishment or religious worship. The Romans used it for a dreadful reason: fun. Hundreds of thousands of slaves and captives were tortured to death simply because Roman citizens found their last agonies entertaining.

A people that finds amusement in watching slaves and prisoners fight to the death, savage beasts tear apart and devour dozens of victims at a single matinee, is not likely to be held spellbound by pretty posturing and catchy rhythms.

Before the vigor and sincerity of the new Christian teachings, such behavior could not stand. The people were fed up. They turned where there was faith and hope, and they put themselves under restraints and cleansing disciplines. No Christian convert was permitted to dance. Ritual dancing was slowly driven from the church with other questionable exercises, like blood sacrifice. It sought unblessed refuge in the fields and town squares.

The Romans in colonizing had enslaved whole peoples, had killed their rulers and destroyed their governments, but the Romans were careful to build their temples on the sites of local shrines. They held their festivals on heathen festival dates (this was not too difficult—harvest festivals and celebrations of summer and winter solstices occur at the same time in the same hemisphere no matter what the religion) and for the sake of good feeling, they tried to preserve any local customs that did not interfere with their own political and military plans. Our May Dances today, our tra-

The Emperor Augustus, c.10 B.C.

Angelo da Fiesole's Last Judgment, *detail, 1425*

Ruins of the Colosseum, Rome, A.D. 70- A.D. 82

ditional Christmas and midsummer celebrations are a mixture of Roman festival and primitive rite. But it is impossible to say now which is which—what steps or customs are the result of homesick legionnaires fraternizing with the local Barbarians and what, if any, are purely Roman dances.

The Christian Attitude: The Christian brought new ideas to the world: that before God, all men—king, rich man, poor man, and slave—stand equal; that before God, women and children are valuable; and that good lives are more pleasing in God's eyes than conquest or achievement. Long before Christ, the Buddhists and Confucians believed these things, but the West did not know about them and held quite a different set of ideas. Even in Christendom, women had few rights in government or family, but before God they were considered to be equal with men. This attitude affected all Christian art, particularly dancing.

When Christianity conquered the heathen tribes of Europe and Asia Minor, missionaries followed the Roman custom (and most of the early missionaries were Roman) of building their churches on heathen shrines or temple sites and using for Christian Holy Days the times of heathen celebration. They borrowed many useful things from older religions: the bell, candles, incense, and dancing. But gradually, under the instruction of the Church, the people began to pretend that the dances were just harmless games. They were instructed not to believe in magic anymore. This was hard. Magic is an old habit. We are still dancing the heathen magic.

The English Morris, performed lustily on the village green, the sword dancers, where the flat flexible sticks that symbolize the swords are woven during the dance pattern into the "lock" or "knot"

43

and then held aloft in triumph, is all that remains of an ancient, prehistoric blood sacrifice. Long ago the "knot" was the head of the victim and the pretty climax to the dance was far more grisly and dramatic. This exchange has proven both economical and comfortable to the performers. Whether or not the ultimate effect is as exciting is another matter.

At the time of the winter solstice, the time of terrible fear, men jumped and stamped on the earth to reawaken it, to call back the dead, and sometimes they wore bells and beat drums and were called Moresco, Moorish, or Morris. But they were actually pre-Christian and they shouted and screamed and made all the racket they could. And do we not still do this with rachets and horns and bewitched, intoxicating singing?

The English Maypole dance (in fact any Maypole Dance) is a fertility ritual, but it is now performed as a game and a courting dance. However, it still is done throughout Europe and even in America, and a breath of the old wonder may cling, the superstitious feeling that it would not be a proper May without it, that our forefathers did it, that no harm can come of it, and possibly some good. The May spirits of England and Germany, masked in green leaves like the pagan priests, still beg gifts. This custom persists like other very old magic gestures: knocking on wood, for instance, which dates back to a time when men believed that gods or spirits inhabited trees and that wood was powerful.

For many hundreds of years the figures of Robin Hood and his men were incorporated into a midsummer Morris pageant, and Robin Hood was honored, much as Pan was, with dances around a flower-crowned bantpole. Max Beerbohm asserted that these Robin Hood rites were performed in England with "not a less hearty reverence, nor a less quaint elaboration, than was infused into the rustic Greek rites for Dionysus."

The old gods showed a spirited resistance to dying, but they were no match for the Christian Church.

Dancing was a formal part of the Christian service and litany until the 12th century A.D. when the early theologians, feeling that dancing was distracting and too often suggestive of impious and worldly ideas, began to root it out of holy ritual. Even the church festivals were purged. The Feast of the Fools, which had replaced the Roman Kalend, had always been a time for lax behavior, and priests turned their vestments inside-out and wore masks. In 1207, the Pope forbade the clergy to wear masks, and in the 15th century the mask was driven forever from the sacred precincts. On special festivals, such as Christmas, dancing by boys and girls had been permitted before the Christ Child on the altar as late as the reign of Henry VIII (1509-1547), but after that only the barest remnants remained in the gestures of the Mass.

The reason for the dismissal of dancing is easy to understand. Christianity taught the subduing of the flesh and the fulfillment of the spirit. No matter how lofty the idea behind any dance, it always involved the human body with all its weaknesses and excitements. The mind wandered from God—or so it was thought at the time. Dancing was accordingly banished, and only ordered processions and marches were retained.

Many of the old pagan figures were retained, the hobby-horse or man-animal, the centaur, sometimes a dragon; the man-woman figure or pagan priest, sometimes the

The Shakers

Music and acting went out with the dance, but music was allowed back later under strict surveillance. Certain branches of Protestant Christianity, the Calvinists, including most New England Puritans, went so far as to believe that all dancing of any kind anywhere was sinful and a direct trap of the devil. There are thousands of people living in America today who still think so.

The Christian Church was the first and only great church to ban dancing from its ceremonials. Christian dancing, as a result, lost caste. The techniques of music, architecture, and painting, luckier in every way, were fostered. But dancing was denied all respect and was cut off from its greatest source of inspiration and protection. It grew to be a despised and frivolous form of expression.

Three Christian sects, all in America oddly enough, produced certain variants of religious dancing: the Holy Rollers, a branch of the Negro Baptist Church; the Holiness Sect; and the Shakers. But their influence did not spread beyond the narrow confines of their own groups.

"'The Holy Rollers,'" says Alan Lomax, "... fought the Baptists and the Methodists with the weapons which they once used themselves. The Holy Rollers jumped, talked in 'Tongues,' went into trances, danced the holy dance and above all reintroduced the old-time shouting spiritual into the church service. Not only that, they welcomed into the church all the musical instruments which Baptist doctrine hold to be tools of the devil, and a new red-hot jazzy musical service emerged which has made the Holiness movement the most popular folk church in America."

The American Shaker dancers were altogether more formal. Beginning late in the 18th century as similarly spontaneous expressions, the caperings and mime gradually evolved into handsome patterns of prancings and retreats with formal bowings done in soldier-like ranks to unison singing. The men and women danced at the same time but in separate groups, and never touching. These marchings and bowings and the pantomimic acts of rejoicing at the bestowal of the heavenly "gifts of resurrection, reunion, and forgiveness" were the principal part of the Shaker service. The steps were as simple as Shaker furniture and dress, and like them the formations were finely designed. They were apparently moving to watch. The restrictions of the order were sufficiently severe, however, to guarantee the destruction of the sect. Among other matters absolutely forbidden were marriage and child-bearing, and conversion unfortunately did not keep pace with the death rate.

The great entrenched churches, the Roman Catholic, the Greek Orthodox*, the Church of England (Episcopalian), the Church of Scotland (Presbyterian), the Calvinist, Lutheran, and Quaker, were to set their faces against religious dancing. It was excluded from accepted ritual and for 800 years the European Christian has danced only for courtship or entertainment. The old pagan ceremonies might still be performed in the village squares, but it was without understanding of their significance. The Church had stolen even memory.

bride but always played by a man. All these dances and rites were performed clockwise, matching the passage of the sun, as they had been from the beginning.

*The Greek Orthodox does permit ritualistic promenades led by the priest at the marriage service.

French Shepherd's Dance,
Book of the Hours, *15th century*

Wedding Dance by Pieter Bruegel, the Elder

Medieval Europe

The peasant dances in existence throughout Europe today are probably more or less what they were a thousand years ago, and use the same basic patterns.

Over the centuries the national forms varied in quality and detail. The English, for instance, were an island people and lived crowded into walled cities, but they knew a greater degree of political freedom than any other contemporary group. They were feeling their way century by century toward democracy, toward a concept of the rights of the common man.

In their longways country dances there is no top, no bottom, no leader; all take the lead in turn and each group has an adequate and equal chance. And in some of these dances for the first time the men's and women's roles are interchangeable; they do the same steps and are equally part of the same pattern.

Furthermore, England was a garden land without any great natural hazards or barriers. It is no surprise to find that in English dances the essential element of design is in ground pattern, open and large, and that free, light running is the preferred style of steps. The "Dancing in the Checkered Shade" that Milton wrote about were simple interlacing figurations, run gently in light, equal steps. (These were the direct ancestors of the American running sets.) There was no fancy ornamentation of footwork or hands. The least effort possible, the simplest, and most direct gesture were desired in all dances. Except in the Morris dances, which were for men only, there was no big jumping. The clogging was simple. There was nothing like the solo stunting by the men that goes on in nearly all Slavic and Germanic dances.

The Germans stamped and slapped; the Russians squatted, spun, and leaped; the Spaniards clacked, clicked, and tapped.

The Village Dance by Rubens

From country to country steps varied, but they maintained certain European characteristics: the body was upright, the arms were extended, and the legs and feet covered space. The dance was outgoing, vigorous and free. This was not true of dances in other parts of the world.

We know exactly what these old dances were like. Folk dances change very slowly—and recently we have started to make searching studies and records of them.

In the last decade of the 19th century an Englishman, Cecil Sharp, began collecting and notating English folk songs and dances. Societies sprang up to discover and revive these lovely old relics. There was a renaissance of folk dancing throughout the British Isles. Great festivals were held annually in London. Sharp came to America and did the same service in New England and the Southern mountains, where there were remnants of the English tradition. The Country Dance Society of America was formed, and now has many practicing groups which zealously preserve the old forms. Square dancing is one of the better modes of courtship and for this reason is widely and enthusiastically practiced.

Now in all countries—European, Soviet, and Asian—there is an awakened interest in folk forms, a zest to maintain this unpolluted treasure as a vital part of the national heritage, a realization on the part of creative artists that it constitutes the ultimate source and repository of all style.

In the East the dancing has been preserved in religious institutions and in a theater more traditional and formal than ours. But in the West, this re-evaluation of folk forms is new, less than one hundred years old, and due directly to Cecil Sharp. In most countries these studies are now government sponsored. Annual competitions like the Highland games, the Irish Feis, the Yugoslav and Czech Sokol keep the dances exact and well performed.

English Maypole dance, c.1840

From "Dances of England and Wales" by Karpeles & Blake, publ. by Parrish, 1950

Cleveland Museum of Art,
Purchase from the J. H. Wade Fund

Root Comparisons of East and West

Dancing in the Far East reached a high degree of subtlety and beauty long ago, and the ancient dances have been preserved. All social and religious classes and castes valued dancing, and through its manifold forms every need and emotion was expressed. The Asians still perform without great alteration the dances they did 2,000 years ago.

Because of the hardships and hazards of traveling, intercourse between the East and the West was continuously interrupted, and thus the influence of one culture on another was limited. The Romans seized captives, slaves, wild beasts, food, and gold, but few ideas. Later, the Crusaders and merchants brought back silks, spices, and gunpowder from the Orient, but unfortunately were unable to transmit music and dancing, there being no means of recording either. The Oriental forms were therefore not available to the West until this century and had no influence on the development of our style or point of view.

The Asians for thousands of years have been hemmed in and imprisoned by religious, social, and economic restrictions. They seldom broke out or ventured forth from their circumscribed fate. The women lived and died for the most part as slaves. The dances reflect the curtailment of physical life. They also mirror tremendous inner searching and spiritual discipline.

The generalizations hereafter stated both apply and fail to apply to Africa. Africa embraces a vast collection of cultures and the residues of cultures superimposed and corroded to reveal older civilizations so that the most startling varieties of period development and cross relationships are found, and characteristics which seem to contradict one another combine frequently in a single style. Many of the quite primitive people who have the attributes of Stone Age civilizations boast also the most exquisite and delicate use of the hands and approach in subtlety Indian and Javan styles. Barefoot savages have an ear for rhythm most Europeans lack, alas, and men who hunt lions with homemade bows and arrows and have never sat a horse, unaccountably leap and prance higher than most Cossacks. Africa has been invaded again and again. Egypt can be traced down the east coast; Rome down the west. It has until recently been called the "Dark Continent" and was left empty of markings on all maps. Nevertheless, people have come and, if they left no history, they left impressions. The people of Africa were not cut off from outside influence like the primitives of North and South America and the Philippine Islands. They cannot be labeled as belonging to any specific stage of evolution, but evidence residual characteristics of many.

For the purposes of the chart on the following page in general it can be said that where the body is exposed and not covered with clothing, the muscles of the torso, of the back, shoulders, and chest are brought into play. This statement holds true for north central and western Africa, parts of India, and the Pacific Islands. It is less true for the North American Indians. Where the body is covered, there is less concentration on spasm and contraction of torso and more on the extension of the limbs and the pattern in space.

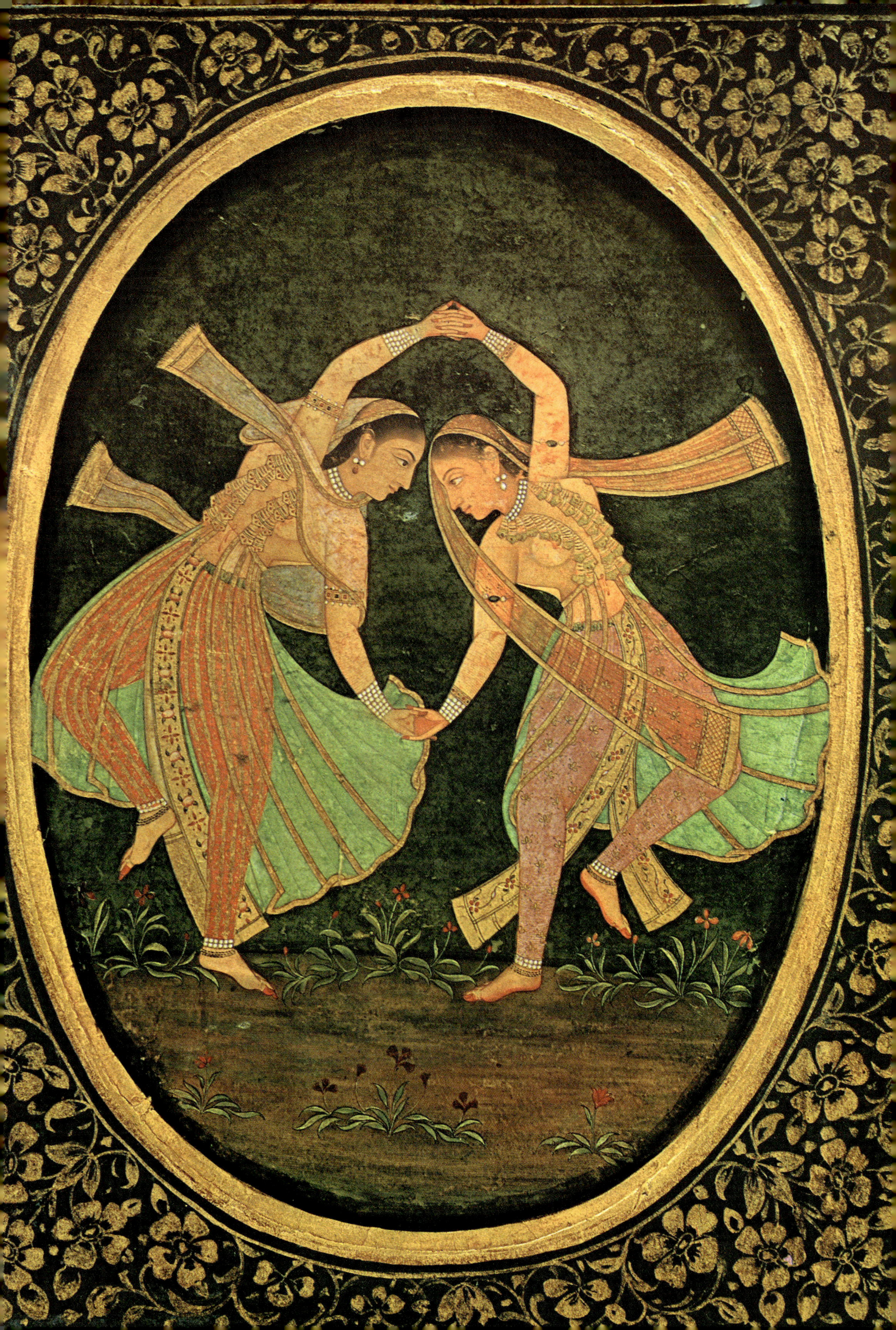

For every statement in this table of comparison, there can be named exceptions, but, on the whole, they are true. They apply to the sophisticated and evolved forms of dancing; the primitive forms in both hemispheres are basically alike.

Among the Pacific Islands and the Far East

1. The dances cover little space and are often performed stationary or seated.

2. The ground is used as an integral part of the pattern; the dance is rooted. Most Asians, the Japanese in particular, can lower their knees to the earth, slip down in prostrating bows, and rise again by pushing on their curled-over toes, without the slightest difficulty or show of effort—a simple daily habit practiced since birth and quite outside the powers of most Westerners. They also squat easily and restfully with the heel on the floor for hours at a time. This practice gives them a heel like a kangaroo and makes the use of the ground in their dancing an easy and frequent adjunct.

3. The pattern and rhythm are contained in the sphere of the body.

4. Natural facial expression is avoided. Every expression is prescribed even to the direction of the eyes.

5. Little jumping or elevation is used. (The Africans jump, notably the Watusis, but not in the straight-limbed leaps developed by the Europeans.)

6. The hands speak with marvelous subtlety and with a language and technique of their own. Great Oriental dancers practice hand techniques as pianists practice finger exercises.

7. The hips are moved, the spine ripples, the shoulders shake.
   The Mediterranean, the Balkan, the Central African, and the Southern Asiatic produce every gesture through flame-like quivering ornamentation or undulations.

8. The knee is nearly always bent, the Achilles tendon stretched, but the foot seldom arched. No big leverage muscles are used and the legs never lifted or suspended. In Indonesia the flexing of the knee is restricted to what will not disturb the wrapping of the skirt. Revealing the underarm or the underthigh would be considered a vulgarity if not an indecency. The Japanese raise their arms, but they are always heavily clothed.

9. He dances for the most part barefooted, or in soft-soled shoes, or foot stockings.

10. Men and women seldom dance together, particularly in aristocratic dances.

11. Men and women rarely touch.

12. Most Asian women, except for priestesses and prostitutes, never dance publicly at all.

13. Costume, make-up, and decoration are dictated by tradition. The Asians have always striven to hide individuality, whether in ritual or in theater, in clowning or in games.

14. Little encouragement is given to creativity or departure from tradition. A repetition of the old forms with absolute correctness is the goal.

From Dayal. "Maipuri Dances, Laya Lahara." Oxford University Press.

Europe and its colonies The Americas

1. The dances cover space.

2. The ground is used as a point of departure; as a surface for space design. The dance is unrooted and free. The dance may contact the earth for inspiration and power (this is what the English "stepping" means: the recognition of the ground) but it is detached and mobile and frequently lifts into the air.

3. The pattern interest lies in the space, or floor design and the interweaving of bodies.

4. Facial expression is ignored or left to natural feeling.

5. All kinds of leaps and kickings are developed.

6. The hands are held passive, on the hip, on the skirts, at the sides, at the neck, or joining, and holding handkerchiefs.

7. Hips, shoulders, and spine are quiet—the farther north the quieter. In the dancing that developed northward through Europe to Scandinavia and Finland, or the North American continent, hips, arms, shoulders and heads seem to get quieter. The Irish, for instance, move nothing but their feet and legs, the Scotch are extremely formal, the Swedes are serene and quiet, while Eskimos hardly bend at all but just clump around in simple stamping and shuffling figures. Costume, of course, may account for a lot.

The Northerner tends to expend his energy vertically, in the air, or laterally over the surface of the earth. He reaches out over ground and air in direct, simple movements, frequently circular and from the waist out. He stretches.

8. He straightens his knees. (Man is the only mammal able to straighten the hind-leg.) He arches his foot and dances on half-toe or tip-toe. Arms and legs are raised and thrown about to their utmost muscular limitations. Big leverage or lifting muscles are developed in thigh and back. Enormous extensions, lifts, and kickings are practiced.

9. He dances in shoes which permit stamping, tapping, and audible rhythms.

10. Men and women dance together in all courting dances on all levels of society with considerable freedom and sense of equality. The farther north the greater the equality. The farther north the more important is woman's position in the home. In warm climates men can get away from the house and stay away with little discomfort.

11. Men and women join hands, link arms, or rest hands on shoulders and waists.

12. Women dance publicly.

13. Great personal freedom in costume is permitted; make-up and even masks are by personal choice.

14. A much greater license for individual invention is granted, particularly in America, where new forms are welcomed with delight.

Shinto priestesses in religious dance

Thai dancer

Where the terrain is easy underfoot, as in open spaces, grassy lands, or sand, one finds running, leaping, and prancing. Where it presents difficulties, as in forests, jungles, or bogs, the dances are much more constricted and rely on rhythm and circumscribed gesture for effect. This is demonstrated in Africa: the northern desert tribes and the sea coast cultures jump and run—the inner central groups do not to any great extent.

In the Orient, on the other hand, although all these varying conditions are present, the enormous complexity of culture, social restrictions, and etiquette have compressed the dance styles to the last degree of precious exactitude, and broken their freedom. There is little liberty in the East, little space, little opportunity to launch forth on one's own. Natural tendencies were long ago curbed and forgotten. Environment is, of course, just as much social and spiritual as topographical and climactic.

THE Eastern and Western styles met and merged exactly at the point where the two cultures clashed and fought it out to the death: in Spain, in southeastern Tartary, in Turkey and Yugoslavia to a less marked degree, and wherever the gypsies traveled.

Gypsy is a corruption of the word Egyptian, but the gypsies were actually Indians. Their Romany language is related to Indian Sanskrit. They kept and carried many of the customs and ways of their ancestors.

They traveled all over Europe as coppersmiths and fortune-tellers, and wherever they went, even in the English Midlands, we find in dances the brilliant oriental use of the hand, quivering shoulders, bending spine, and jerking hips. But the gypsies held themselves outside of law and kept apart, refusing to mix. In Hungary and Russia their influence was perhaps greatest, in England and Spain least. The Spanish Gypsy or Flamenco (which literally means "Flemish" but which pertains to the southern gypsy) has a different origin. The flamenco, together with all Spanish dancing, derives from the Moors.

The African Mohammedan, or Moor, is our only direct link with the East. For over eight hundred years (612-1492) he settled by the hundreds of thousands in Europe. He inherited his art and literature from the Persians and his religion in part from the Hebrews and Christians. He believed in one God and in one great prophet. Like the Hebrews, he believed in revenge and his own race. Like the Romans, he believed in conversion by the sword. His civilization was in many ways advanced for his age. He gave us algebra, the numerals we now use, astronomy, medicine, plumbing, and engineering.

His dancing reflected all the Eastern aspects of the Mediterranean. The men's dances were fraternal or religious, frenetic, repetitious, acrobatic. In his civilization, women had no standing, no voice in law, no hope for heaven. They lived in harems, or great coops, the voiceless property of their men. When they went out, they covered themselves with thick veils. They sang and danced only for their own diversion and to please husbands, fathers, or brothers, the only men they were ever permitted to meet. Street girls were permitted to entertain in low coffee houses or wine shops, but they were outcasts.

Men and women never danced together; in fact, they never went out to parties together. Even at home the women did not eat with the men. There was no such thing as a family dinner.

Women never performed religious dances. There were no dancing priestesses among the Moors. Mohammed said that Paradise would be full of dancing girls, but the Mosques on earth were scrupulously kept clear of them.

The Moorish or Mohammedan dancing had many of the characteristics of the oriental form. To these were added certain African embellishments, a heavier shaking and trembling of the shoulders, a rotating and jerking of hips, the snapping and crackling of fingers, and muscle dancing.

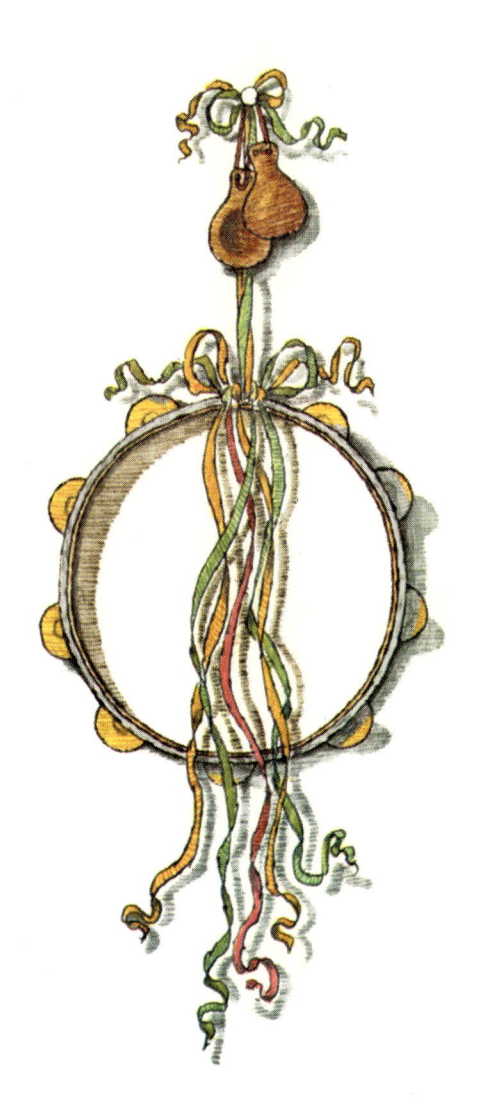

The Moors in Spain

Dancing Girl *by J. L. Jérôme*

The Bolero *by Doré*

All around the Mediterranean basin, including Algeria, Greece, Armenia, Turkey, Egypt, and Israel, the dancers employ a lateral sliding of the neck back and forth on the shoulders. Among the Moroccans, Algerians, and modern Egyptians, there developed also techniques of dancing where the hips and shoulders remained relatively quiet and the muscles jumped and rippled. This, while unacceptable to most northerners, is common among many tropical people. It is called muscle dancing and is considered attractive by those among whom it is practiced. There are well-known stars in this technique as in others. A virtuoso can do such astonishing things as place one full and one empty glass on her naked belly and, by giving thought and a well-placed twitch, overturn the full glass into the other.

For almost eight hundred years (711-1492) the Moor infiltrated Spain, establishing cities, universities, agriculture, commerce, developing engineering, plumbing, science, and arts. As far as he conquered in Europe, the African Moslem influenced or dominated architecture, music, and dancing.

In 1492 the Moors were driven from Granada, their capital and their last great European stronghold. But much of their way of life was absorbed by the several million people they had associated with. When the Caliphs left Spain, one million Moors—artisans, shopkeepers, and peasant farmers—remained behind. These had to live with Christian ideas and customs, and from this union the classic Spanish dance was born.

In this dance, in the inward concentration and self-absorption, in the encircling arms and the undulating hips, in the supple bending spine and the formal use of the eyes, in the manipulation of veils, draperies and skirts are found a mysteriousness and seriousness authentically Oriental. But there are also found the jumping, racing, and the beating of feet, the bounding leaps of the Basques; the castanets and tambourine embellishments of Greece and Rome; and a brilliant technique of heel and foot rhythms that is the Spaniard's own invention. Waldo Frank, in *Virgin Spain*, writes:

"In the hands of the Gitana the castanet is—as perhaps it was in the Dionysian rites—a heightened bloodbeat to the music.... Here it is an instrument subtle as a voice....Like the arabesque— a decoration evolved from the written language—it retains an intellectual power. The music of the castanets is apart from the dance. While the arms flow like birds wheeling, while the body becomes a throat of song, here is analysis forever present."

The Spanish women knew the grace and allurement of the East, but the Spanish women were Westerners and Christians. They lived more freely. They danced at balls and at court and they danced with male partners. Muscle twitching stayed on the other side of the Gibraltar Strait; the Spanish have none of it. Nor do they uncover their bodies. They cover up, with veils, gauzes, and fans.

"Sinew of the North confronts the fluid South," says Frank. "Two dominant forms embrace in warfare: a music, hurried like prayer, rhythmed like heartbeat, and this fierce coldness on a woman's body....The dancer is a column, articulate of spirit: a live plasticity: with the moods of eye and waving hand flung like a largess to our sense."

Opposite the Alhambra, the Caliphs' great palace in Granada, are the caves of Sacre Monte where the gypsies live. Their dances follow the pattern of all other Spanish forms except that they retain the Moorish music almost unchanged and the techniques of singing in quarter-tones and falsetto, the Oriental finger-snapping, twisting of hand and wrist, and a jerking of hips and bend-

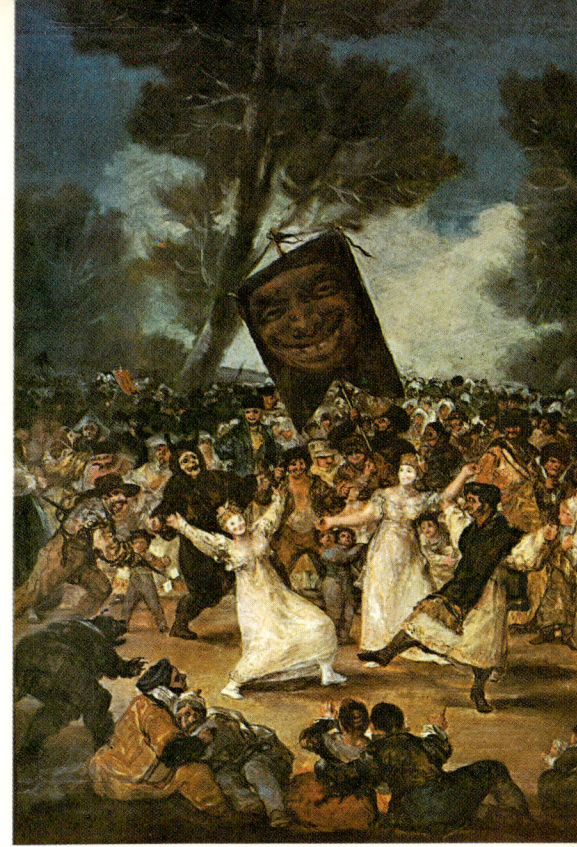

From "Goya" published by Skira, Geneva-New York

The Burial of the Sardine, *1793, by Goya*

El Jaleo, *c.1899, by J. S. Sargent*

Isabella Stewart Gardner Museum

Dance of the Gypsies, *1862,*
by J. D. Becquer

ing of spine that is more pronounced than the classic Spanish style permits.

The gypsy men and women dance like tigers. Matched in strength and brilliance, they dance together, but they do not perform the same steps. There is a highly developed distinction between the steps and manner of a woman's dances and of a man's. For this reason there are always romantic overtones to their dancing, more so than in English or Danish folk dances.

The style evolved gradually as a dance for single figure or partners and is rarely danced in groups. As in all folk forms, the men and women seldom touch even when exhibiting the most startling virtuosity. Classic Spanish dancing, whether flamenco, popular, or court, with its complex rhythms, elaborate heel taps, and castanet patterns, has developed a technique way beyond any contemporary popular form in Europe and requires years of practice to perform even passably well. Most good Spanish dancers begin as babies dancing right along beside their fathers and mothers, learning castanets and the use of the skirt and heel almost before they can speak.

Dancing is taken seriously and cherished in Spain—and because it is cherished, it is of high excellence. The Spanish dance deals chiefly with courtship and bull fighting, which is partly a ritual blood sacrifice and partly a Dionysian rite.

Dancer from Carmen Amaya's troupe

Robert Inesta, Jr.

The Spaniards were the last Christians to give up their religious dancing and they did so reluctantly. Yet eventually, like all good Catholics, they had to obey church edict. In Jaca, in Aragon, and in the cathedral of Seville, the only remaining dance choristers of the Christian Church, "los Seises" (literally "Six"—but now ten boys), still perform a slow sarabande on Easter week and clash castanets before the altar.

"The Spanish dance is organic and essential." Again we turn to Frank. "It is the one great classic dance surviving in our modern world.... Since it is a true classic art, the need of personal genius to express it is reduced; the true genius here is tradition.—Spain dances."

Spanish Dancers, painting on tambourine by Manet

Courtesy of Lillian Moore

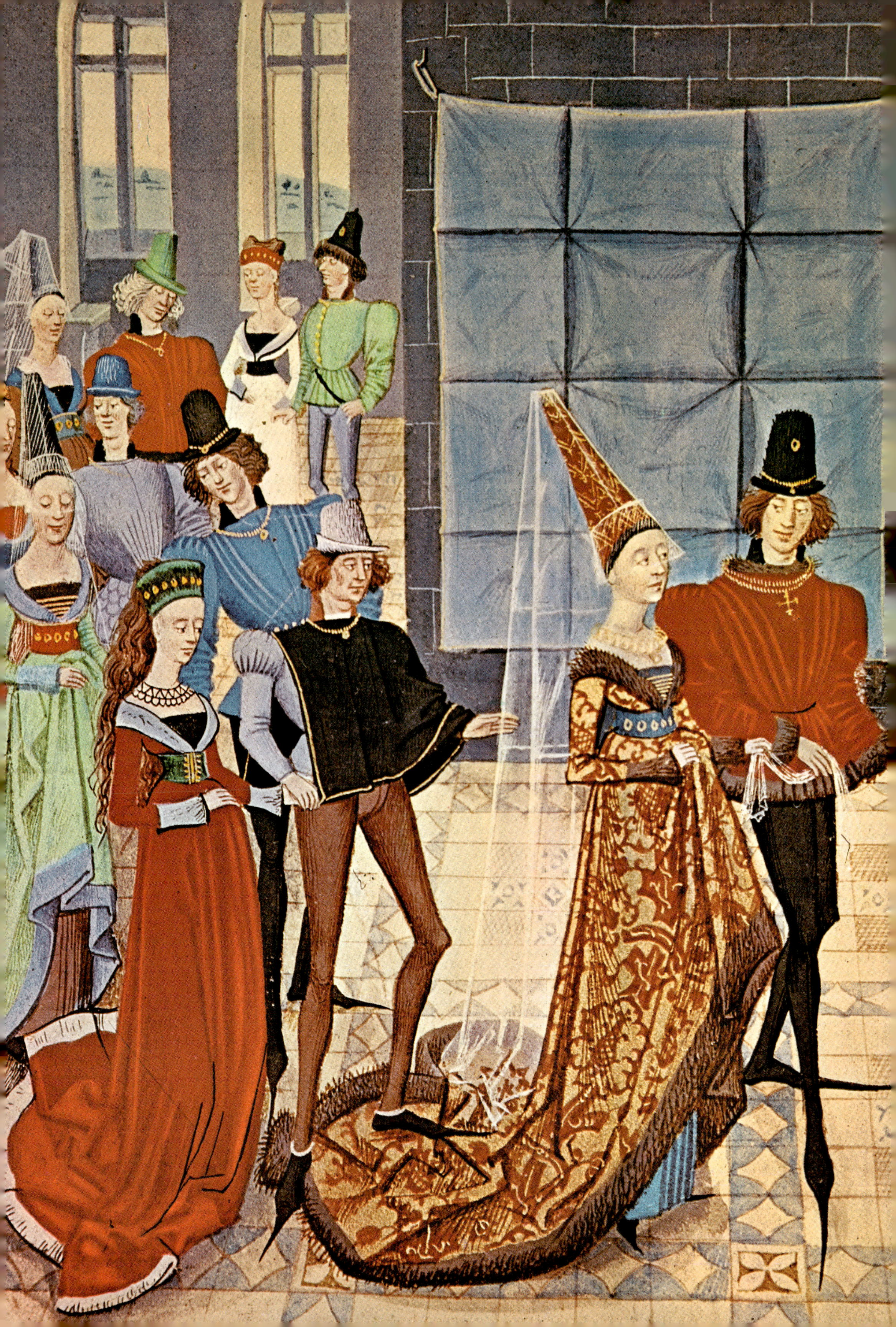

E ACH country in Europe had its own variant of the basic social dances. The courts, however, developed them into elegant forms. Because it was the rich noblemen who traveled, these forms were practiced universally in all court circles as fast as they could be learned. The patterns were adapted from peasant style, omitting rough steps and horse-play.

Court dances were concerned almost exclusively with showing off and with courtship. And for this reason, dances for couples gradually came into great favor.

The Medieval courtier was a figure of consequence; he thought himself better than anyone, except for men of higher rank and, if he were devout, the clergy. The king looked up to no one except the pope and not always to him. The pope looked only to God.

Every one of them—kings, nobles, and clergy—could kill men of lesser rank with no more than a casual excuse, and with little or no punishment for doing so. England was the first country to say that the common man, although not fit to stand erect or be hatted in the presence of a noble, nevertheless should not be killed without a formal explanation. Until that enlightened time, any baron had the right to test the blade of a new sword on the first peasant he met; his servants existed not as human beings but as conveniences. Equals killed each other, with and without rules. When there were rules, it was called jousting or battle. When there were no rules, it was called murder. There were no police forces. Relatives took action in the case of murder, except, of course, the relatives of poor people.

The courtiers lived by birthright and power. They loved beautiful things and they had the money to build or buy them, or the force to snatch them. They grabbed everything they could. Their lifelong game was a competition to see who could get the most lands, the most castles, the most horses and jewels, and the most noble wife with the most lands, castles, horses, and jewels.

These mighty men were not always able to read and write, but they were smart and, above all, they were proud. They made a cult of pride. It was called courtly behavior.

They set great store by honor and loyalty and courage, and by keeping the rules of their killing, grabbing, and showing-off games. These were all part of courtly behavior, or chivalry. Chivalry was a substitute for police, written law, and centralized government responsible to the people. It worked well; it worked as a conscience.

The Medieval Man, the Feudal Man, was deeply religious. The noble felt himself responsible for all the people who depended on him. If he had power of life and death, he had duties, too. Part of his pride and honor derived from the care he took of the dependent and weak. Among the weak he classed all women.

Love-making was practiced as a kind of art and the etiquette of courtship was highly developed. Chivalry included the near-worship of a beloved person—not necessarily one's wife.

Bal à la Cour du Roi Yon de Gascogne, *15th century*

Alinari/Art Reference Bureau

Medieval and Renaissance Dances

Lorenzo de' Medici by Verrocchio

Unknown Florentine

Accordingly, all the arts of high coquetry were in their dances, the use of handkerchiefs, fans, veils, long trailing skirts and cloaks, posturing and stamping, spur-clicking, and preening. When one of these great war lords walked down the floor before his king or his lady, you can be sure he did not aim to be overlooked; however simple his steps, he did them full out. Indeed, he must have presented quite a spectacle just standing around.

Imagine then simple folk steps, the European folk dances we know today, danced with this point of view, and you will get an idea of what the court dances were like.

This is a Renaissance courtier. He was a great warrior, on horse or off. He brought to dancing the legs and feet of an athlete. He wore no heels—just soft leather moccasin-like shoes. He could, therefore, do many things ordinary gentlemen today cannot do, not even tennis players or track stars. Getting through a day of his routine activities gave him the legs of a marathon runner. A full suit of iron plate armor weighed about 50 pounds, the two-handed sword up to 15 pounds, the battle helmet from 3½ to 5½ pounds, the jousting helmet much more, the tilting lance 12 to 20 pounds; and he was a small man, considerably smaller than men today.

His armor was Cordoban steel. He was used to armor; he felt safe in it. He extended his arms wide. He made sweeping gestures and exposed his body, something no primitive would do.

His carriage was upright and free. His hands were exquisite, for all that they were used to handling heavy weapons. It was the mark of a gentleman to have fine hands.

His lady always dressed in heavy low-necked robes and elaborate head gear and jewels, even when getting up in the morning, even when supervising the housekeeping or visiting the nursery. For a ball she wore such heavy-cut velvets, tissues, and jewel-encrusted silk that she sometimes fainted. These dresses had long trains, so the dance steps could not be much more than gliding, tapping, or posing. These were called Basse Danses or low dances. It is safe to suppose she swayed her hips a good bit since she could move little else. Indeed, the priests were continually scolding her about the indecency of doing just this. When she nodded or swayed her head, her gauzes and jewels winked and twinkled.

There were "haut" or high dances, also. They were supposedly jumped, but probably ladies, clad as they were, merely hopped and let their more nimble and strong-legged partners take care of the elevation.

In the early sixteenth century dances began to be skipped and stamped with heel beats in the Spanish style. Heel beats presuppose heels and shoes with stiff soles. The soft suede moccasin boot of medieval Europe was discarded, for streets were now paved with cobbles and were hard underfoot. Removable clogs had always been used to keep fine shoes out of the mud. Heels were permanently added to the sole to give the foot of both men and women elegance and the whole body stance a superiority and spring. A great iron two-handed sword could not be manipulated in heels; the new lighter one-handed rapier or dueling blade could.

The Spaniards knew about leather. They made the best boots in the world. The Spaniards also knew about steel.

N.Y. Public Library Dance Collection, Cia Fornaroli Collection

The dance of Salome, 15th-century engraving

Morisco Dancer *by Erasmus Grasser*

They conquered parts of Italy, the Netherlands, and the New World. They attacked France and England repeatedly, and left behind governors and minor courts, stranded soldiers and shipwrecked sailors. These accidental immigrants taught their neighbors Spanish dance steps and rhythms. The rounded Moorish encircling arms found their way into the French, Italian, and Hapsburg courts, and so later into ballet. The leg and foot beats were imitated everywhere, but simplified because the northerner did not have the Spanish ear. Might not the Irish clog, so intricate in rhythm and so unlike anything in Scotland or England, have been the happy issue of celebrating Armada victims and bog-dwellers? "He stands moveless.... Suddenly, his feet break in a shattering tattoo from which his body rises in subtle, suppressed waves. His arms...are still at his side, or they are held in fixity near the shoulders. The body is vised: the head does not swerve. Feet and legs make a dance, perpendicular and juiceless;...they bespeak the hoof-beat of armies, the vigils of the desert, the absolute symbol of the Arab Darwish."—so Waldo Frank describes a Spanish zapateado, but he could be talking about an Irish jig.

In far-off England, in an attempt to mask pagan ritual with Christian history, the Moorish or Morris Dance, called the Matachin, tells the story of a battle between the Moors and Christians; they dressed in ribbons and bells and one of the performers always blackened his face. "These light beribboned Sons of the Soil,"

Munchner Stadtmuseum

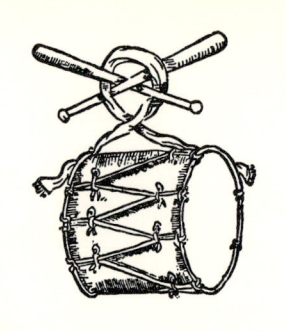

Illustration from Orchésographie *by Thoinot Arbeau, 1588*

writes Max Beerbohm, "were hardly less glad in their dancing than was that antique Moor who, having slain beneath the stars some long-feared and long-hated enemy, danced wildly on the desert sand, and to make music, tore strips of bells from his horse's saddle and waved them in either hand while he danced."

In pueblos once controlled by the Spanish conquistadors, the San Ildefonso Indians of New Mexico perform today "Los Matchinos," as knights riding horseback to conquer Seville.

With the coming of heels in the 16th century skirts shortened throughout Europe and dances that were jumped and scampered like the galliarde (Cinque Pace, Shakespeare's Sink-a-Pace or Five Steps) appeared. The men began to devise waggings of the leg, crossings of the feet in mid-air, and capers (the little goat step or capriole, now called in ballet a cabriole).

The ladies, being in shorter skirts, might be supposed to have had an easier time of it, but they were also in iron corsets, and farthingales, or boned wheels around the waist. They continued to wear cut velvet and taffeta silks and pearls and precious stones that weighed up to forty pounds for each costume. Nevertheless, they jumped and pranced and tapped their heels on the floor in a frisky and elegant style. Elizabeth of England, although ailing all her life, prided herself on dancing all the most difficult steps. The men devised a way of swooping the lady up in the air, sitting her comfortably on the man's knee (the volta). It had to be a strong thigh and knee to bounce a lady together with considerable iron and whale-bone and a good part of her father's fortune. But these men were used to ten hours straight in the saddle.

La Gagliarda, 1611

Queen Elizabeth I, anonymous, 16th century

National Portrait Gallery, London

62

The invention of firearms changed the emphasis in many aspects of living. Whereas before brute strength and endurance were the prime virtues of a soldier, now speed, intelligence, forethought, and alertness counted for more. All armor and weapons changed. Warhorses, which had been ponderous Percherons capable of withstanding the onslaught of a cannon, were replaced by Arabian thoroughbreds with the speed of leopards and the nerves of opera singers. These required a new technique of handling. The riders found they themselves had new requirements and deportments.

In the next two hundred years clothes became lighter, manners daintier, dueling more expert, and dancing more skilled.

All courtiers took a dancing lesson every day and their dances were exact and rigidly schooled. They were simple in steps, gracious and pretty and very intricate, involving fancy floor pattern, separations from one another, and changing and lacing of arms. The emphasis was always on deportment and manner and the sequences had to be practiced. There was no vague improvisation as in our modern dances, with the man just pushing and the woman following passively.

The 18th-century courtiers took great pride in the play of instep and wrist and the coordination of arms and hands in counter rhythm to the feet, something only trained theater dancers can master today.

We know exactly what these dances were from graphs. They were not in the least like the stage minuets and gavottes we commonly see, a sort of pat-pat-peek under the arms. These are fake

An Easy Introduction to Dancing by George Bickham, London, 1738

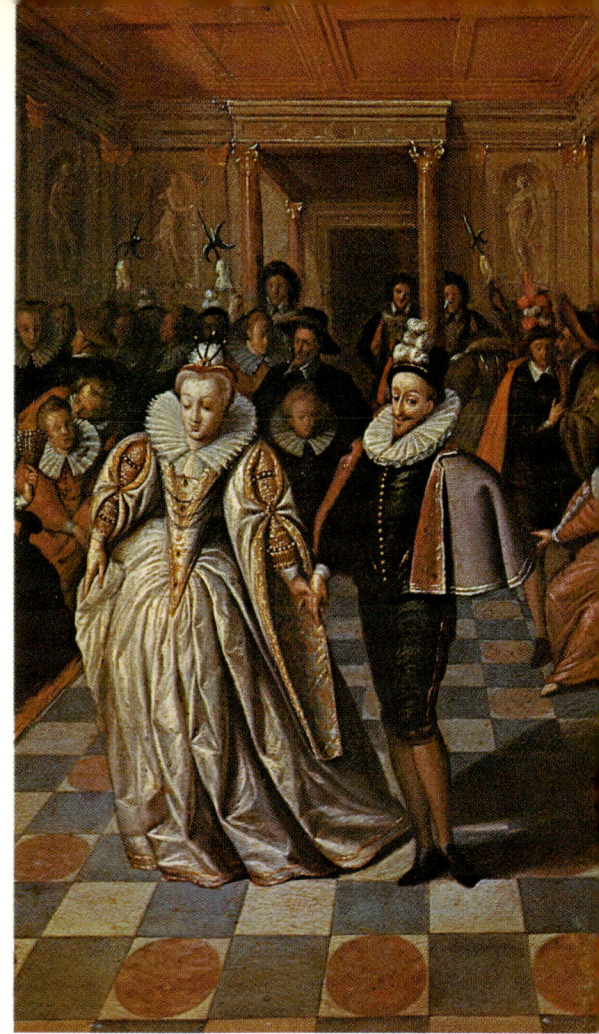

Bal du duc de Joyeuse, *François Clouet, 1581*

The French Art of Dancing by Kellom Tomlinson, 1735

A description of the correct method of waltzing, the Truly Fashionable Species of Dancing by Thomas Wilson, London, 1815

Music cover, c.1840

N. Y. Public Library Dance Collection

dances and were devised for 19th-century actors who could not possibly perform the real steps. They are dull, stodgy, and pointless. We must never forget that no one has ever at any time done dull dances for pleasure. These are invented only by untalented people for money.

Our common ballroom position is recent. Nothing equivalent is to be found in any primitive or ancient dance. It was first introduced in the 16th-century volta and was then considered indecent. In primitive or peasant communities men and women barely touch hands, sometimes insisting on the further antisepsis of a handkerchief held between them. Some European dances boldly allow the men to put an arm around the girl's waist in order to lift or spin her around. Very occasionally he is allowed at the end to kiss her. These kissing dances have always been understandably popular. But peasants have never danced face to face, body to body, clasping one another tightly as we do.

The volta became the waltz in the 19th century and although frowned on, gained in favor.

In the 19th century the formal, delicate, and intricate social dances of the 18th century, with their patterned sequences, their interlacing but respectful positions, and their dainty steps—the minuet, gavotte, passepied, gigue (or jig), courante, rigaudon, allemagne—gave way to simpler and more intimate forms, the waltz, the polka, and the mazurka. These were peasant dances from various European countries performed with elegance in the ballroom. They could be altered or improvised at will. There were a handful of group dances with set figures—the Paul Jones, the lancers, the polonaise, the german, the quadrille—which also derived from the peasant forms. But these were used mainly as grand marches to interchange partners.

The folk dances have continued without basic alterations down to the present, the social dances making the circuit from village square to court to middle class drawing-room and back to dance-hall. Since 1850 there has been little invention or change in Europe. The last new popular European dance was the French Can-Can which began in the cafés in the late 1840's. This was probably the first truly urban folk dance. It was a rough and vulgar dance and reflected the vicious environment in which it was conceived. It involved continuous high-kicking, the raising of skirts, and was not accepted as suitable for ladies and gentlemen. It became the exclusive property of the dance halls and was taken over by professional girls who could kick exceptionally high and jump into splits.

Since the introduction of the Parisian Can-Can, all the innovations have come from the United States, and Cuba, or South America.

Bibliothèque Nationale, Paris

The Waltz in 1840, from a lithograph by J. David

N. Y. Public Library Dance Collection, Cia Fornaroli Collection

G. Cruikshank, 1817

American Social Dances

EVERY group of people that has lived on this continent, even the Indians, anthropologists tell us, has been restless and explosive in expression.

The settlers found plenty of dancing wherever they went, but they paid it absolutely no mind. Indian dancing was the goings-on of heathens and savages and generally preluded trouble.

The settlers took kindly to tobacco, corn, potatoes, leather-work, and furs, but to none of the art forms. This was a pity because the Indians had much to teach us. The races shared little except firewater, gunpowder, and scalping knives, a poor basis for any kind of cultural exchange.

The people who came to America brought their own dances, but by far the most preponderant, in influence as well as pervasiveness, were the English forms (the country dances, longways, and rounds). But here the tripping sets were raced; there was more room. And here they were shouted; there was more energy.

The European dances underwent little adjustment to the new environment except that they spread out and became quicker, longer, and harder and were performed counterclockwise; some of the dance sets lasted fifteen minutes of steady running. They had to be strong people who stayed the course. And they were. They led hard lives.

Women were scarce; women were valuable. The dances were always gallant.

They were also democratic. Every dancer had an equal chance. There were no solo passages except in a "hoe-down" or dance competition in which the first one to miss step lost out. There was no top, no bottom, and no "presence" (the word for the king or ranking noble) as in all European court dances and in many European folk forms. The dances were called or shouted by a leader, always a man, much in the fashion of English longways sets, but the instructions here were developed into a humorous comment. These were "called" or whined at unbroken speed not only to cue the performers but to throw caustic and spicy insight into the manners of the community. Good callers are famous.

"Runnin' up the river Indian style,
  Ladies in the lead and the gents plum wild."

"Give your arm to your girl
  Give your arm to your honey
  Double up boys
  Get the worth of your money."

"Gents to the center and back to the bar,
  Ladies to the center in a right-hand star."

And as a signing-off and finish:
  "Well you know where
    And I don't care."

These are still our country forms, current in all rural districts.

People in polite society and in the cities followed the example set in European drawing-rooms until the new indigenous forms began to take over. But these were most unexpected.

Dance Magazine

American square dancing, 1840 and 1940

Gloria Bercielli, Country Dance Society of America

In the 17th and 18th centuries over eight million African Negroes were imported as slaves. They came from a wide variety of territories and represented many kinds and degrees of culture. These people brought with them a remarkably developed sense of rhythm and body technique, unlike anything the European had practiced. The use of the naked foot, the body rhythms, the endurance and ecstasy were akin to the American Indian approach, but whereas the Amerindian danced for power and magic control, the colored slave danced for escape and forgetfulness. And since he had no entertainment except of his own devising, he danced for fun.

The Indian danced toward spiritual integration, the marshaling of his powers for endurance and ordeal; the Negro (here in America) danced for release, abandon, and comfort.

The Negro has changed much of our art expression, particularly in music and dance. The Indian was kept apart from the white settlements and was, except for brief interludes, hostile. He was either feared or despised, certainly never copied. The Negro lived on the premises and sang and danced before the house steps, in the yards, over work in the wash houses, the bake houses, the weaving rooms, and the forge. The white children watched, picked up the rhythm, and joined in. The white child's nurses and playmates were Negro. He was instructed more deeply by them than anyone realized. A new kind of lilt took over in songs and dance, the accent was placed, not on the downbeat as in Europe, ONE-two but on the upbeat or offbeat one-TWO. This was African; it became American.

Rhythmic beats began to be missed and the accent slipped to unexpected counts. We call this syncopation. While it was known and practiced by great musicians before, it was not generally used

67

The Old Plantation, c.1800, anonymous

Jazz improvisation by Covarrubias

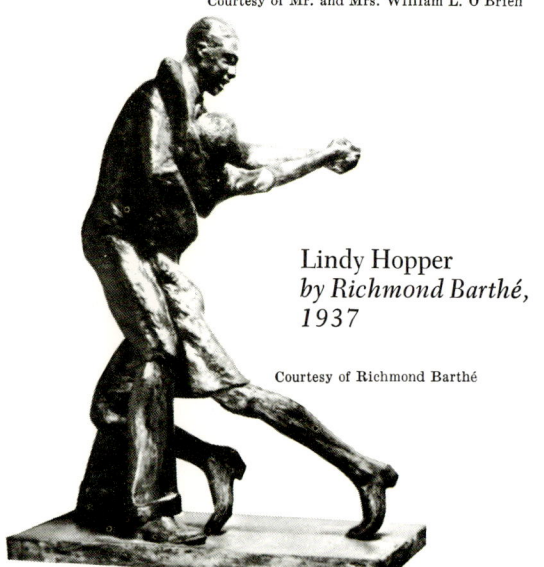

Lindy Hopper by Richmond Barthé, 1937

in Europe by ordinary people. The Americans now clapped and stamped their dances on the offbeat.

After an unsuccessful but alarming uprising of slaves in 1739, laws were enacted forbidding Negroes to use drums, their native instrument, for any purpose at all, even for dancing. The slaves transferred the drum rhythms, the message-giving rhythms, to their feet. They rattled tambourines (borrowed probably from the Spanish Creoles of the south), they clacked bones together like castanets. They changed the *bonja,* an African gourd with strings, to the banjo. It became their stringed instrument. It is native American and it is found nowhere else in the world.

By 1830 they had developed a highly complicated and brilliant form of rhythmic dancing, brand new and their own. They let go, in body, in face, in voice, in fun. And while they danced they yelped, called, giggled, laughed, and moaned. This was a great lesson to the white folks who had been taught that ladies and gentlemen did not yell or wiggle when dancing. The Negro folk danced better, with more personal expression and invention, and the Negroes enjoyed it.

In mid-nineteenth century there was another tremendous immigration, this time by the Irish, who came voluntarily but in desperation. They came by the thousand because there was a potato famine at home and whole villages were starving. The Irish tinkers traveled everywhere in the south in encampments and they performed their jigs and reels and clog dances wherever they went. The foot rhythms delighted the Negro slaves who learned them quickly, changed the Irish downbeat to the syncopated off-rhythms, added African emphasis, the free loose swing of body movement. The Irish dance permits almost no arm or body movement; the head and torso are held rigid. The Irish dancer seems to live only through his feet, in a starved, rocky kind of way, rooted into the ground, beating defiant tattoos on the bare earth (they frequently clogged at the crossroads where the ground was hard and without grass). The Negro threw away all such restraints. The decorous hornpipe and Irish clog became the exuberant American buck and wing, tap, and jazz.

Since then, every ten years or so, from the slums, wharves, the Negro ghettos and impalements, comes a new contribution to our folk vocabulary. Their creativity never ceases and their flair for performing makes the dances popular. Their body rhythm and frank sexuality turned the formal European waltz into the closely clutched two-step and one-step, the cake walk, fox trot, Balling the Jack, the Charleston, the Black Bottom, Varsity Drag, the Lindy-Hop, the jitterbug, the shag, the Susie Q, the Big Apple, rock 'n roll, and the Twist.

These dances were in a sense rougher, less respectful, less kindly or gallant than any other courting dances. They were developed in low and unsavory dives by desperate people. Reformers kept referring to them as "African" or "Jungle" or "Primitive." They were, of course, nothing of the sort. This dancing was developed by a captive race working under the false conditions of the cage. All captives show the marks of their torture. In the roughness and lack of courtesy, these dances are degenerate, but on the other hand, they are full of invention and rhythm and humor.

The Turkey-Trot and Bunny-Hug actually were devised by a white man, Joseph Smith, the son of George Washington Smith, our first great ballet dancer. He watched Negroes at work and copied body positions and rhythms, performing the finished steps first in vaudeville. They were later taken up as social dances all over the country and for a time became the ballroom vogue.

These steps, whether invented or inspired by Negroes, are as original and as expressive as the gavotte or minuet, but their most unusual aspect is the rapidity with which they develop. The English and French required 250 years to change the Elizabethan volta to the waltz. This exuberant and prolific people produce a new form each decade. No other racial group boils up constantly in such rich spontaneous gesture. The fact is the Negroes have not lost the gift of improvisation as we have, and use it in all their art and social expressions.

At the beginning of the century Joseph Smith and Vernon Castle and his wife, Irene, invented many new steps and advertised them in public exhibitions of ballroom dancing. They performed in contemporary clothes, not in costumes, and they were the first people in 150 years to do this. Although professional entertainers, they made up dances to be copied by ordinary people and to be danced everywhere. The Castles were marvelous performers, inventive and tasteful, and they changed the style of social dancing over the western world. They popularized the one-step, the fox trot, the Castle Walk, and glide; from South America they introduced the maxixe. The South American tango, another closely-clutched, body-to-body dance from the Argentine dives, had already been introduced by Joseph Smith. The Castles cleaned it up and popularized it.

Collection of Nickolas Muray

The Jitterbug by Covarrubias

The Charleston danced by Joan Crawford

Famous ballroom dancers of the early 20th century. Irene and Vernon Castle and, at extreme right, Florence Walton and Maurice.

The Castles' music arranger was a Negro, Ford Dabny, who had been the official pianist to the president of Haiti. He helped them change the old 19th-century rhythms to the syncopated, brisk, and gay Negro jazz beat. The old social dances, the waltz, the german, the schottische, and polka, rapidly became less popular. They are as obsolete as hand-made buttonholes or plackets. Very few people today can waltz well, even highly trained theater performers.

The Castles were followed by a number of fashionable dancing couples, among the most notable, Maurice and Florence Walton, Maurice and Leonora Hughes, Tony and Renée de Marco, Moss and Fontana, Veloz and Yolanda, Fred and Adele Astaire, Fred Astaire and Ginger Rogers. These were predominantly performers, not inventors; nor were they as influential as the Castles. However, they did reintroduce the idea of adults going to dancing school to learn proper dancing manners and styles, and while no one today takes social dancing as seriously as did an 18th-century courtier, flourishing businesses have been built up on the schools.

Irene Castle was svelte, light, and graceful and looked so much more attractive than the overstuffed, pudgy women of her generation that she made dieting popular. She refused to wear the artificial and uncomfortable corsets that had been stylish in one form or another since Queen Elizabeth I. She unlaced. She wore light girdles and knickers, and full floating skirts of light materials. She was not the first woman to do this, but she was the first fashion-

70

Museum of the City of New York

Social dancing in 1963, by Susan Perl

able woman to do so. She was considered the best-dressed woman of her time and she set the style for the western world.

Women no longer fainted all over the ballroom. The free-striding Castle Walk with the woman's arm lightly resting on the man's was the march toward emancipation. No woman in a hoop or bustle could have moved this way. The man still led—with the woman going backward—but the entire body posture, spread of step, speed and zip, belonged to the new century, with new standards of grace and seemliness. This was more natural, more vigorous, and less artificial than any dancing done by gentlewomen in four hundred years.

With the exception of our running sets and squares, our courtship dances today are nearly all couple dances and improvised without pattern or rules, something that an 18th-century lady or gentlemen would consider disorderly. The two-step, the fox trot, the jitterbug (a very rough dance), rock 'n roll, the Twist, or more recently The Slop and The Pony, are not so much dances as steps and indeed are somewhat difficult to tell apart as they involve no set body positions or relationships and permit great informality and caprice.

One significant contemporary development is that the partners, as in primitive decorums, tend to keep separate, not touching, even with fingers, and frequently not even looking at or speaking to each other. They jig on in a kind of self-hypnosis with a barely acknowledged and silent shadow beside them mirroring their energy. It is solo performance done in multiplication. Relationship has all but disappeared; a dance floor today is not a group of couples but a crowd of individuals moving in concert.

The individual is no longer part of a cooperating group or community, as in the laced 17th- and 18th-century forms, or as in our country dances; he is now a separate and lonely figure working entirely on his own without plan. There is a growing tendency to reintroduce the traditional squares which are, because more interesting in pattern, much more fun to do. They are also much more gallant, and even the beatniks are beginning to recognize a need for courtesy.

The new forms have been taken back to Europe, and Negro and Latin rhythms and steps are fashionable from Stockholm to Port Said. The Europeans are inventing no new dances, nor is anything coming out of the Orient. The Japanese and Indians and Turks and Egyptians are accepting our forms. Since they never did social dancing in mixed company, the newly unveiled women have had to borrow our steps, their grandmothers having no suitable ones to teach them.

Spain alone seems impervious. The Spanish peasant and gypsy like their own way of doing things. The flamenco dancer would probably consider a rhumba or the Twist flat and silly—and compared to his own beautiful dances, it is.

But swing and bebop with their accompanying steps captivate the rest of the world from Tokyo to Cairo, Tel Aviv to Los Angeles. The Americas have become the great factory for dancing, which means that our culture is growing and changing and is in this respect extremely healthy.

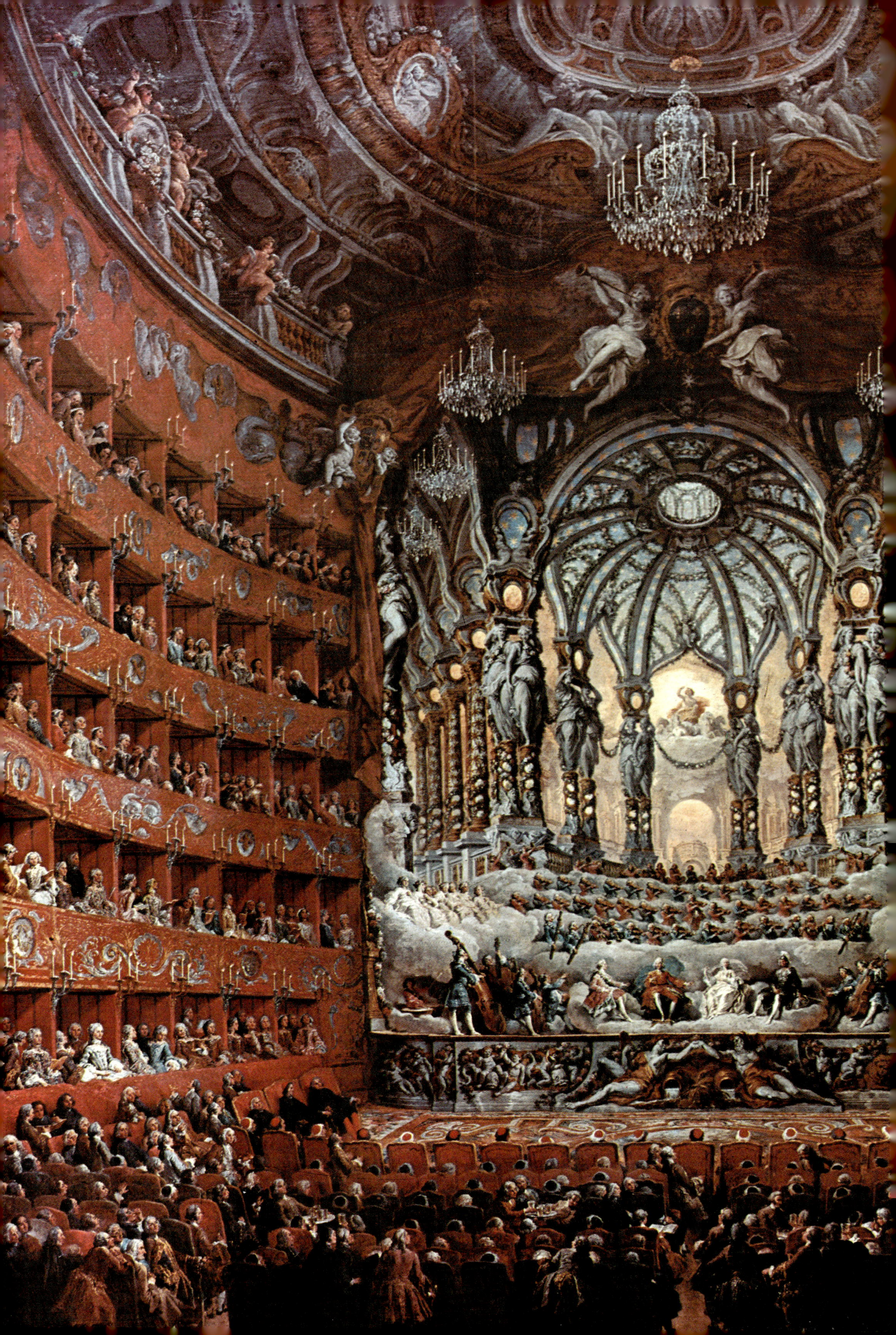

Book II

THE THEATER AND BALLET

The Rise of the Western Theater

ALL the dances hitherto discussed—for worship, for courage, for food, for fertility or courtship—had one characteristic in common: they were designed to please the dancers, and only the dancers. They needed no audience, no spectator, no critic. Success was measured in the satisfaction of the people who did the dancing.

But in theater the dancer is now merely an intermediary or agent. The spectator gets his emotional benefits by proxy. Anyone can now live through enormous experiences without the wear and tear on his own life and without some of the dreadful practical results.

A young girl no longer needs to be really sacrificed by her father at the spring rites; Iphigenia is killed symbolically in a play, and all fathers and mothers and daughters have the benefit of the experience without the effort.

The entrapped and bewitched princess is freed from unpleasant circumstances and finds her true mate—but no young lady watching need disobey father or husband to know the joy of romantic fulfillment.

People like most to watch what they wish they were themselves doing. When they see a good representation, they experience almost as deeply as if they were truly living out the episodes.

Aristotle called this living and experiencing by proxy "catharsis" —the freeing, exercising, and cleansing of the emotions. All theater is based on this, even theater that attempts only to make us laugh.

Theater always reflects the culture that produces it; strong creative periods have fine theater. The reverse is equally true. No theater at all means a poor, starved kind of living.

When ritual becomes entertainment, actors are no longer gods or demons—they are not even priests, they are intermediaries. They remind the audience, they teach, they record, but they have lost their magic potency.

The characters in any theater, as before in all rituals, divide into two categories:

(1) The gods, ghosts, or heroes, who wrestle with fate and the forces of life. These are the characters of tragedy.
(2) The common men who make mistakes, the imps, half-gods, satyrs, fauns, and impious spirits who act as intermediaries between men and gods, men and Fate, who encourage men and cheer them up. These are the characters of comedy.

Every race that produced plays has stories dealing with both kinds of characters.

All great civilizations have had theater except the Jewish and Mohammedan, both of which barred any depiction of God or saints, and accordingly forbade the use of masks and imitative acting. Both cultures had dancing and singing for entertainment, but not composed dramas or spectacles. Nor had the Egyptians any theater as we use the term. It was the Greeks who gave us our tradition.

Oddly enough, although the African Negro used masks, figures, and totems in all his religious rites and sacrifices, he somehow never made the transfer from blood ritual to theatric substitute.

The Watusi, who have a royal ballet of trained professional dancers, are the exception to this statement. These trained dancers function during court festivities. They are called "The Thoughts of the King." The King himself no longer dances; he sits in state and watches his proxies perform.

The primitive Greek drama consisted originally of choruses and dances celebrating the mystic death and rebirth of the god Dionysus.

Although later the Greek plays were written by professional playwrights and performed by trained and rehearsed actors instead of priests, they retained many of the characteristics of the old ritual before the god's altar; the danced and chanted service, the sacrifice (the hero who is killed), and the rebirth of the god (the new king).

The plays were not, however, entirely religious in purpose. Their function was partly moral, to warn and instruct, and partly emotional, to rouse and release the feelings—catharsis.

The playwrights competed for prizes each year at the spring festivals. The performances were open to the public, held in great open amphitheaters that were used for nothing else, that were, in short, the first proper theaters.

All the gestures were stylized. The plays were written in verse as artificial as opera. These were chanted, often with musical and dance accompaniment. The amphitheaters were large, so the actors were shod in great high-soled shoes to increase their stature, and they carried big masks. These masks made the characters identifiable at a distance, and the mouth of each mask contained a megaphone.

These were the practical reasons for the use of symbolism and mask; there were deeper ones: concealment and suggestion. As people found out long before in ritual, symbolism is more emotionally moving than realism. What is imagined but not seen grips the heart most strongly.

And as helps in suggesting what can only be hinted at, men used dance steps, music, poetry, masks, and costumes that put a spell on both performer and audience because they said, as though with trumpets or the bringing in of lights, "Now, at this moment, this is true. Believe this!"

From time to time the audience was asked to believe unlikely and astonishing things. Gods or great ghosts were not apt to appear on earth as common men, and no Greek god ever did, nor could he, look like a common actor. There were only three actors in each tragedy playing the many speaking roles, but they had a wide selection of masks to choose from.

The mask is "The face that represents many men rather than any one man," says Walter Kerr. "...[To-day] we do not care much about the universal image...we like to see the individual countenance of individual actors—personal, idiosyncratic, and unique. Perhaps we have become too private and too special, and so lost something." But in Greece they were dealing with universals.

Pierre Martinot

The actor, to be effective, like the priest or the modern psychoanalyst, must never be thought of as himself. He must be recognized only as the character he says he is. The great actor wishes nothing, certainly not his own history or personality, to get between his purpose and the audience, not, at any rate, while he is working. He cannot play two parts at once—himself and the role; he must never become his own rival. He must be transparent, and for this reason, throughout the history of the theater, he has seldom used his bare face. Even today, in our stage and screen, he uses artifices and disguises that have become symbolic. The great actor, like the great musician or dancer, disappears in the performance.

Clowns have always in every country worn or painted on false faces; for if the real man fell flat or got continually hit on the head, the audience might not laugh so hard. Punch and Judy look like no one you ever saw. Even Charlie Chaplin wears a sort of mask; without his mustache and trousers, he is unrecognizable on the street.

The Greeks, too, hid their faces and never showed violence or outrage realistically on the stage, but rather suggested these things through symbol. They believed that intense emotion must be veiled to be endured. If the meaning behind a tragic act is to be felt, the act itself must be suggested, not shown. Raw grief, open horror—a street accident, for example, or murdering torture—was, they said, merely shocking without being saddening or elevating. Pity and horror were what they sought to arouse, but never horror alone. The Greeks were very strict about this. They might perform blood sacrifices in religious ceremonies, but, though their tragedies were dreadful, even involving the slaughter of whole families, they allowed no visual brutality in their theater.

The same restraints presumably applied to dancing—no violence, no contortionism, no vulgarity, no sensationalism, but rather harmony of line, fine rhythmic effects, and dramatic power.

The great Greek tragedies were largely mimed and danced. And if dancing performed such mystic and poetic service in such high company, it must have been good. As a matter of fact, it was the playwrights themselves who invented the gestures. Aeschylus is credited with devising wonderful new rhythmic movements for his chorus. In all probability the theater has not had choreography of like dramatic effectiveness until our present era. Our own great dance dramas are but now evolving. We were to travel a long and tortuous path. After Greece we in the West went abruptly downhill.

The Romans in their entertainments, as we have seen, were neither self-respecting nor respectable. All theater, and dancing with it, was given over to brutality, horror, sensuality, dangerous acrobatics, and vile clowning.

Rome had, for a short time, robust comedy, and some of this influenced later drama. The actors in Roman comedy, like the tragedians, wore masks. There came to be traditional types or stock masks: the glutton, the miser, the rascally servant, the hero and heroine, which were carried down through the miracle plays to the 16th-century Elizabethan drama and the half-improvised Commedia dell' Arte, and thence, much, much later, into opera bouffe and ballet. But on the whole, Roman theater and dancing were sensational and brutal.

The Christian church, having seen in the arena and circus what Rome considered entertainment, decided there would be no more of that sort of thing. All Christians looked upon the theater with deep loathing; it symbolized depravity and horror. The Church permitted none of its members to act or dance and finally slammed the theater doors shut. The great open circuses were used as stone enclosures for market towns, and people built half-timbered and thatched houses into the tiers of seats like swallow-nests. The names of Sophocles and Euripides were unknown to twenty generations of men. The music was forgotten. For a thousand years there was no theater in Europe. This was during the time of medieval Christianity, called, for sound reasons, the Dark Ages.

But the theater is essential to life and the Church has never overlooked a good thing. After the first Crusades religious plays and episodes began to be performed in the church naves, then in the courtyards, then by the guilds in the town squares and on great rolling wagons that went from place to place entertaining and edifiying the audiences at various crossroads, or stands. These plays were called mysteries because they dealt with the mysteries of the Old and New Testaments. In dispersing the Roman mimes through banishment, the Church had spread their comic tradition throughout Europe. There was a great deal of lively acting and clowning in these spectacles, but dancing played a small part, and was restricted to improvised gambolings by workmen and guild apprentices. Women were not admitted to the guilds and therefore presumably took no part in the guild plays.

Of course, there was always dancing in the streets by trained animals and acrobats. There were strolling players ready to give a show at any crossroads, and there were gypsies. Nearly all of these were banned by law from decent towns and many a dancer hurried away under a rain of rotten eggs and dead cats. "No beggars, mountebanks or actors," said a sign on the town gates.

Actors for centuries were classed with vagrants and thieves, and dancers were considered even lower, for they smacked directly of the devil. No gentleman would have anything to do with the theater professionally. By the 16th century men with gifts or ambition turned elsewhere if they could. Nor were decent or noble women allowed in; in fact, no women of any station. This had nothing to do with women's talents for performing. They have always been good performers. Rather it was because it was thought unseemly for women to appear in public. Good women were kept at home. It was considered damaging to women to let them out of the house, and damaging to the theater to let them in.

"The church was beset by an ever-present fear that the great pagan revels might be revived, unloosing once more the furious pleasures of the flesh and the devil," writes Duchartre in his book on *Italian Comedy,* "and it was perhaps due to this fear that for 16 centuries throughout the Christian world all women were prohibited from acting in the theater."

In the 16th century certain important Italian states, not including the Papal states, lifted the ban and women began to appear

Actors of the Italian Comedy by Lancret, 18th century

18th-century Nymphenburg porcelain representing characters from commedia dell' arte

in the comedy troupes called the Commedia dell'Arte. These women acted, sang, and danced very skillfully.

Prostitutes, who were social outcasts, have always contrived to dance in the low entertainments and cafés, but any woman who became a dancer lost standing. The pay was poor, the conditions shameful. Business managers, designers, and choreographers were not tempted to work for them. There was nothing approaching a dance or ballet company. For all the Christian talk about equality for women, they were treated, when it came to the arts, with almost Eastern restriction.

Even in the heyday of the Elizabethan theater, at a period of expansion and imagination, women were still kept out—boys played their roles. In London, women were permitted on stage only after the Stuart Restoration in 1660.

The playing of women's roles by men did not lower the dramatic standards in any way. The boys were expert and the job, though not respected among gentlemen, was at least considered an honest trade for the unpretentiously born.

Theater in non-Christian parts of the world fared better. In the ninth century, thirteen hundred years after Aeschylus, the Japanese Noh dance-dramas and Gigaku emerged, closer to the Greek classic tragedies than to anything in Europe. A few centuries later across the world, in Peru, the Incas were performing long narrative dramas of chanted blank verse acted out by celebrants in gorgeous costumes, masked and topped with plumes of gold and feathers, while in Mexico, the Aztecs played satires and comedies in verse.

These Indians tragically did not invent the means of preserving their theaters. The Inca and Aztec cities and all they held are weed-covered mounds and their dramas are remembered only through reference in 16th century Spanish letters to King Philip II. The Japanese lyric dramas are exactly preserved, each gesture, each intonation written down and transferred, teacher to pupil, without deviation for 1,100 years. They constitute the oldest unchanged theatrical tradition in the world, and they represent a climactic achievement in poetry, dancing, and music. The Western Christian theater was not to evolve dramatic poetry as fine until the Elizabethans, 700 years after the Noh plays, nor any outstanding musical drama until 800 years later.

In the latter part of the 16th century, Western poets began to bring their talents to the theater. In England Shakespeare, Christopher Marlowe, Ben Jonson, John Webster, and a dozen others; in Italy, Torquato Tasso. There were superb composers as well: William Byrd, Thomas Morley, Thomas Weelkes, John Dowland, Claudio Monteverdi. Great poetic drama was achieved, the beginning of great lyric drama or opera. Nothing like such splendid imagination was brought to the dance.

Theater dancing did, however, begin to develop very slowly, but in the courts, not in the theaters proper. Little by little, there evolved the complex and unique invention, the most difficult, the most unnatural, the most universally popular form of dancing, the flower and pride of our Western theater—the classic or opera ballet.

THE technique and style of ballet has stood like the rules of harmony. It represents one of the longest unbroken traditions in the Western theater. It is as perfectly preserved as any technique in singing or instrumental performing and older than our present technique of acting. Since the time it started developing from country to court performances about 300 years ago it has never been wholly out of style. Today it is more popular than ever before in its history. In the United States alone there are more than four million ballet pupils.

Balletic tradition has influenced all kinds of theater dancing, except American tap-dancing. "Grace" in our language is balletic style. A "graceful" performer, no matter what the type, is a dancer who coordinates arms, head, and hands after the fashion of the 17th-century court dancer.

The posture and attitudes are always noble and controlled, the demeanor of a king. The style is based on majesty—and this is not surprising since only royalty and nobility danced in the early ballets.

The Court Ballet

Every courtier was an able swordsman. If he was not a good swordsman, he was not a courtier

———for long.

Gymnasium of the Academic Arts, *anonymous, c.1690*

Every courtier could dance.

The gestures were symmetrical, harmonious, circular; all opening from a central axis, based on the turned-out leg and *port de bras* or fencing position. He turned out his feet to provide a base for thrusting, dodging, and recoiling. He had to be able to move in any direction instantly. He danced as he was used to moving in all court procedures.

He loved this style in all design.

We know exactly how the princes and nobles looked. Their style and deportment come to us in our ballet exercises, straight from the Renaissance and Baroque Courts of Europe, handed down from one generation to the next. It is in this technique and in a few military maneuvers that we learn how monarchs moved. Consider the strut of the drum major in the Scots Guards. Toe first, with fully extended instep and knee (the courtier's mincing step to exhibit the calf and the jeweled shoe), the legs moving freely from the hip, back and head erect, arms swinging out and flourishing in arrogant confidence. As the soldier stakes out his path with a long staff, planting and twirling it back, we see again the monarch peacocking down marble halls. The walk is artificial yet manly, affected yet elegant. It swings; it never swishes. It is ornate, swift, and commanding. There is a lifetime of discipline behind it. When the drum major steps out before his massed pipers, each toe testing the earth to see if it is worthy to bear his weight, he is confident the audience will rise to their feet or break en masse into cheering. And they do.

The ballerina's grande promenade, toe first, is a variant of the same walk. When she appears on the stage, royalty enters.

It is a 17th-century rigaudon that the Highland soldier performs on the crossed blades of the claymores, a dance learned at the court of France where his kings, the Stuarts, and their families sought refuge on and off for a hundred years (1640-1740). This is the posture, the lightness, strength, brilliance, and cat-like use of the foot that ballet dancers borrowed, and these are the fingers held formally and exactly in the 18th-century ballet position.

We have rejected the political and social ideas on which court life was based, but we must remember that in dancing very nearly all the concepts of beauty and of grace we inherited were created and fostered by the court or by the church. But it was the court, and not the church, that fostered dancing.

All of the courtiers, both men and women, had lessons from childhood in deportment and etiquette.

There had been court ballets throughout Europe from 1400 on, held in palace halls or gardens. They began in Italy; Catherine de' Medici, who became the Queen of France and the mother of three French kings, set the style at the French court. These ballets were pageants, made up of parades and social dances (the court dances were elegant versions of the country dances) interspersed with lengthy poetic speeches honoring a royal marriage or birth, a visit or betrothal, or the successful ending of a war.

Costumes for an equestrian pageant, such as the one below

Bibliothèque de l'Arsenal, Paris

The British Museum

Louis XIV
by Hyacinthe Rigaud

Giraudon/Musée du Louvre

Women of quality first appeared in theatricals in 1681 when Lully persuaded four princesses to brave court etiquette and appear in Le Triomphe de l'Amour.

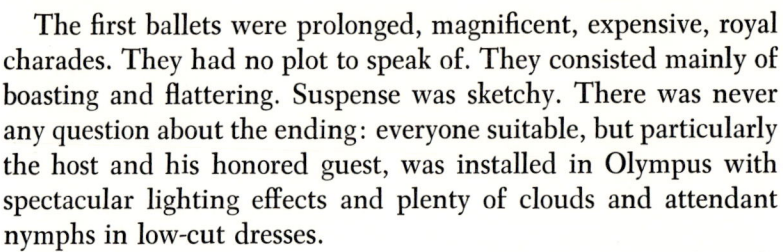

The first ballets were prolonged, magnificent, expensive, royal charades. They had no plot to speak of. They consisted mainly of boasting and flattering. Suspense was sketchy. There was never any question about the ending: everyone suitable, but particularly the host and his honored guest, was installed in Olympus with spectacular lighting effects and plenty of clouds and attendant nymphs in low-cut dresses.

The themes of these masques were either allegories or legends of gods and heroes drawn from classic mythology. Unlike the drama, they never dealt with religious subjects, and they never on any account dealt with real life or contemporary peasants or townsfolk, except as clowns or buffoons.

Louis XIV was not by any means the first king to dance in ballets, but he was the fanciest and the fussiest. For twenty years he took daily lessons from his dancing master, Beauchamps. Everyone took lessons and they were exacting.

Decorum did not slack off for a century and a half. "Your Majesty," said the later dancing master Despréaux, "respect is shown in the quickness with which one sinks to the ground and in the slowness with which one rises, rather than in the largeness of the movement. The bow of an inferior consists in sinking quickly and rising slowly. Contrariwise, the bow of a superior consists in sinking slowly and rising quickly."

Guillemin instructed his students thus in how to receive a dancing master:

"The student—[not the king this time]—should meet the master on his arrival and receive him with fitting courtesy, then make his two bows, the first very low, the second less so; he should then show him into the room and invite him to be seated in an armchair or chair. As soon as the master [lady or gentleman] is seated, the pupil will hold out both his hands, place himself in the first position and make four bows [the knees well turned out], the first very low, the second less so, likewise the other two, taking care not to raise his heels. [This, dear Reader, is very hard to do and the untrained need not attempt it.]

"The bows accomplished, the pupil will walk forwards, then backwards, to the right or left, and in any other manner that the master may deem fit.

"The lesson at an end, the pupil will have the courtesy to attend the master to the door of the room; he will then make his two bows, the first low, the second less so, and politely thank him for all the trouble that he has taken."

What did they learn in these lessons?

The ballet posture (the rotating out of the legs at a 45° angle at the hip), the straight leg, and the special coordination of head and arms (or port de bras).

What did they strive for?

Brilliance of footwork and elevation, or the ability to rise vertically in the air and dance off the earth.

The posture is based on a straight and quiet spine, a stiffened, straight knee (and this is the only form of dancing in the world that uses the stiff knee), and level hip line. The hips may not lift, thrust out, or rotate. The shoulders may not ripple.

The ballet dancer must start training young and continue for hours every day, and may not leave off the daily practice at any time while dancing publicly.

The technique is based on the turnout of the legs and five positions of feet and arms. The 18th- and 19th-century ballet student employed machines and devices by which, as a sort of rack, they turned out their legs. These mercifully are no longer used.

Because we have inherited the eyes of our ancestors, along with their language and manners, we find the long unbroken line to be the most exciting a dancer's body can assume. The knee, except when flexed in a bend, is held absolutely taut and straight. It is never relaxed. The leg is turned out so that the front of the knee and the flat unbroken line of the leg are presented to view—never the lax droopy aspect of the side of the knee. The legs are held in their turned position by the great muscles across the buttocks. The spine is steady. It bends, but it never convulses.

The transitory movement joining the positions is simple, smooth, and outward, opening from a central axis.

An equally important change occurred in the physical presentation. The ballets worked out on ballroom floor and lawn were transported into carefully designed surroundings or theaters.

Habit d'Andimion du balet du Triomphe de l'amour
N.Y. Public Library Dance Collection, Cia Fornaroli Collection

Design for a stage setting with perspectives by Bibiena

Louis XIV's ballets were performed in the stables. His great-grandson Louis XV built a private theater. It was not open to the public. One could not buy a ticket. One came only by royal invitation and the audiences were small. If the king did not clap, no one else was permitted to. One can assume that when royalty danced, applause was liberal. Louis XIV's great-great-granddaughter-in-law Marie Antoinette danced a lot here. They say she was charming and light-footed and that her walk was "swan-like."

The few public theaters there were in Paris were well attended. A pastoral opera *Pomone* with dances by Beauchamps ran in Paris for eight months in 1671 to crowded houses. The cast was entirely of men—no women appeared as dancers on the public stage until 1681. Women—that is, royal princesses and noble ladies—were permitted in the court performances before invited audiences, but never, naturally, in public for paid admissions.

The steps of the court ballets were simple because the dancers were amateurs and because they liked to dress up in elaborate and expensive costumes. Just managing their daily clothes took practice and they wore even heavier and more difficult suits in their ballets. Nowadays, dancers take off all they can. Seventeenth cen-

Louis XIV, the Sun King, as his namesake Apollo.

Bibliothèque Nationale, Paris

Versailles, 1668. Notice that the two great side wings have not yet been added.

Photo Giraudon/Musée du Louvre

Bibliothèque Nationale, Paris

tury courtiers held a contrary view. The supporting of the great trains, the lifting of the stiff and dragging brocades and satins forced the arms into a curved position. The bodices cut low on the shoulders and the sleeves heavy with lace and ribbon limited shoulder movement. The fingers came to be used as though they were plucking up satin even when they were not.

But the costumes, no matter how cumbersome, were good for their purpose. They set off the tiny feet, the tiny and elegant waists, and the superb shoulders and bosoms of the women, and the wonderful legs, insteps, and hands of the swordsmen. They set off the royal spines and the elegant noble heads. Both men and women seemed to float over the marble and silken earth. Some of these costumes weighed as much as 150 pounds, so the steps were kept largely to marching and bowing, or even sometimes riding in formations, and the dances relied on floor patterns for interest. The ballets, indoors and outdoors, were miracles of geometric design and mechanical effect.

Great fortunes were spent on these effects. The *Ballet Comique de la Reine* in 1581, celebrating the betrothal of the sister of Henry III to the Duc de Joyeuse, cost three and a half million francs—in terms of our money today a stiff amount even for a king. The best engineers of each period designed the stage machinery and props, the most famous architects the sets and backgrounds, the greatest painters the robes. In the time of Louis XIV, the engineer who designed the fountains of Versailles devised many wonderful ballet transformations, and Boucher, court painter to Louis XV,

The king watches a ballet

Archduchess Marie Antoinette and her brothers in a children's ballet at Vienna, 1765

Bibliothèque de l'Arsenal, Paris

87

designed satin suits for stage shepherds. The jewels were real, of course, the material Venetian velvet, Lyons silk, and cloth of gold, the horses blooded Arabian, the performers blooded aristocrats.

Everyone loved theatricals and everyone tried to act. Amateur performances were given each weekend at the chateaux and country houses. Many of Molière's and Voltaire's plays were written for these house-parties and performed by the authors themselves and their friends. They also danced and sang original pieces. Their technique may not have been very expert, but their style, as in everything they did, was handsome.

Some ballets went on for six hours. These amateur actors spared themselves and their audiences nothing. But we must remember that these spectacles, together with chamber music and processions, were the only form of entertainment people had. There were few popular theaters, no movies, no television nor radio. So when they went to pageants they liked them to last.

But four hours of marching and declaiming can grow fatiguing. The nobles began to think of conserving their strength. They had a lot of things on their minds—they had hunting and entertaining and keeping in the king's notice—none of which could be done simply. Even getting up and going to bed, or eating supper, and ordering clothes, or building palaces were no easy matters. Louis XIV and XV had, besides, serious religious troubles and several wars. We would call them small wars now, but at the time they seemed quite large enough and were deemed disastrous in terms of loss of wealth and lives.

Such things cut into the time available for theatricals. So it seemed a good idea to call in professional help. The dancing masters and their best commoner pupils were invited to do the com-

The gentleman on the right is a duke and he is playing Apollo; the lady on the left is Venus. She may not look like Venus, but she is a princess of the blood and she chooses to play Venus. He prides himself on the shape of his calf. It will always be in view.
The lady prides herself on her arms, the carriage of her head, and her bosom. They will be in view, too.

N. Y. Public Library Dance Collection, Cia Fornaroli Collection

plicated and tiring bits, and gradually, as professionals will, they took over the show.

The few public theaters in Paris at the close of the 17th century naturally showed marked differences from the court theaters. "When theaters began to be rebuilt in conformity with the conventions of Italian opera," writes Tyrone Guthrie, "not only did the audience and the actors now face one another; a great gulf was fixed between them. In this gulf sat the orchestra, grouped around the conductor.

"This was only partly a matter of practical convenience. It also marked the social chasm which separated the predominantly courtly and aristocratic audience in the stalls and boxes from the socially inferior persons who were paid to entertain them. The separation was reinforced by yet another practical and symbolic barrier of fire—the footlights."

At about this time it became the custom for the dancers to wear masks. It is difficult to imagine why any noble star wished to dim the effect of his personality. Possibly he did not wish to exhibit himself barefaced beside a partner with the rank of a lackey. Louis XIV frequently danced with the composer Lully beside him. (Composers were considered as upper servants, although they were, if distinguished, sometimes treated with fondness.) The ballet teacher Carlo Blasis says the courtiers wore masks because the ancients did, as a part of the traditional costume and style. This was probably not the whole reason. Very little thought was given to historical accuracy, as you may judge from the costumes.

It had long been the custom in European court life to wear masks whenever people went off on a lark or mischievous adventure, into the streets on foot, for instance, or to the theater, or to fairs. In Italy carnivals and disguises sometimes lasted six months; any excuse was taken to wear a mask. Romeo, you remember, when masked was allowed to enter Juliet's house. People habitually admitted without question masked adventurers to their private parties; it was mysterious and fun. Kings and courtiers and caliphs, masked or in disguise, could do things they would not otherwise have been permitted to—and so could ladies. Perhaps dancing in ballets began to come under the general heading of indiscretion. Ladies wore the black half-mask partly for concealment and partly for appearance, to set off their "pearl and nacre" complexions. Courtiers were used to wearing masks, sometimes two at once—the under one a portrait mask, the upper one a fantastic face.

In any case, the wearing of masks in ballets certainly limited the acting, such as it was, and increased artificiality.

In his *Mémoires* Casanova writes of the dancer Louis Dupré in *Les Fêtes Venetiennes* (1750):

"...Suddenly the pit gave vent to a loud clapping of hands at the appearance of a tall, well-proportioned dancer, wearing a mask and an enormous black wig...."

N. Y. Public Library Dance Collection, Cia Fornaroli Collection

This is one of the first professional dancers. He represents a faun. He is neither royal nor noble. He has, however, learned manners. In these plays he walks shoulder to shoulder with princes.

Venetian ladies of quality by P. Longhi

Foto Cacco

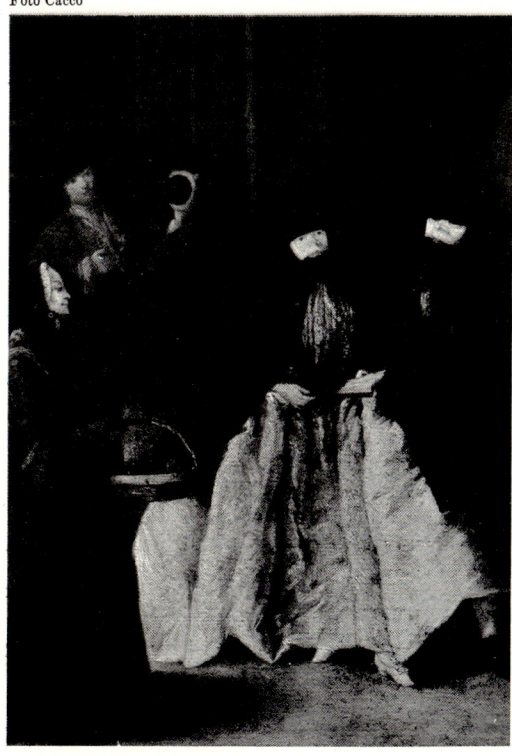

Masks worn by dancers during the 18th century

Musée de l'Opéra, Paris

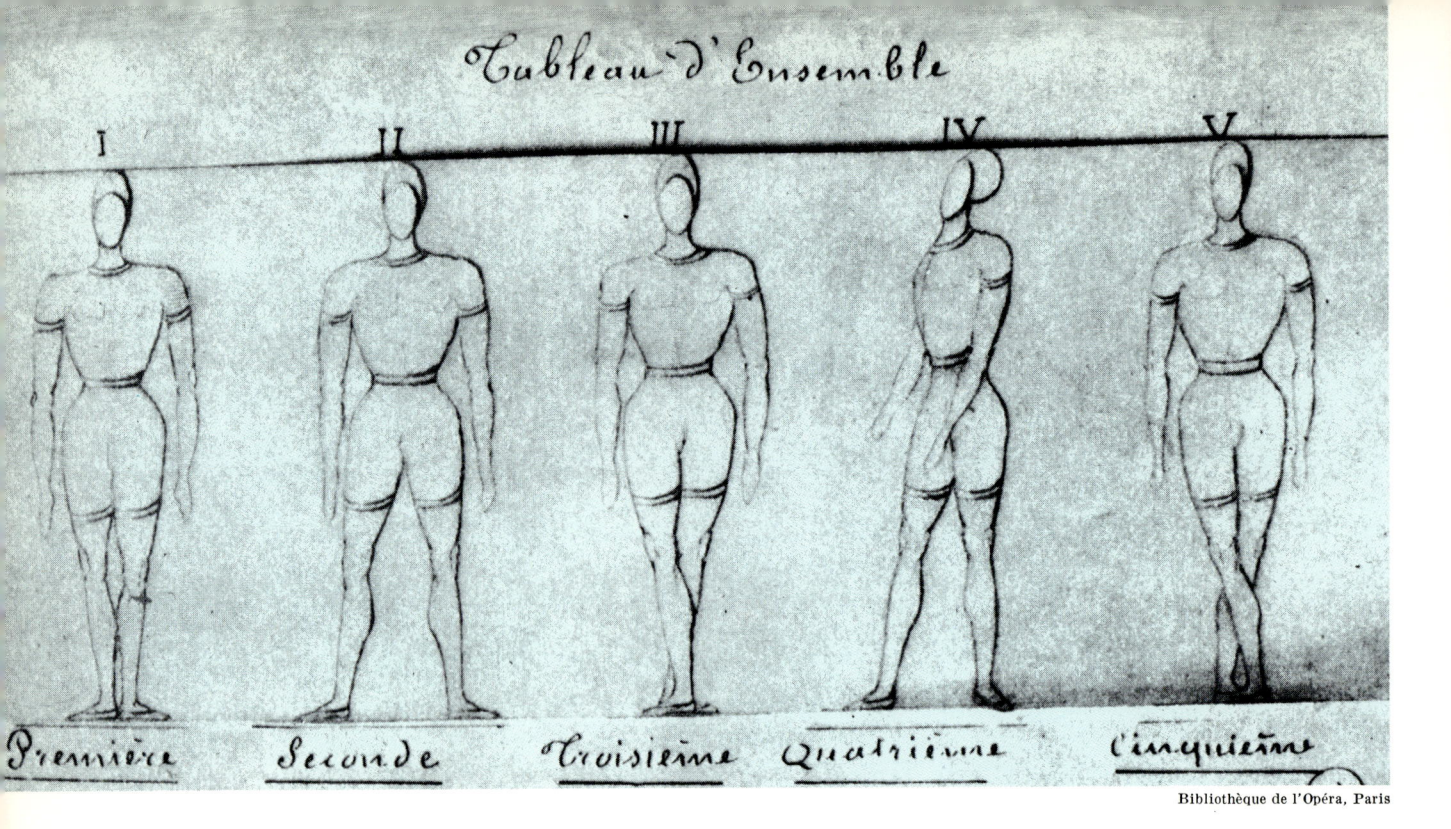

The five classic positions

Choreography for horses

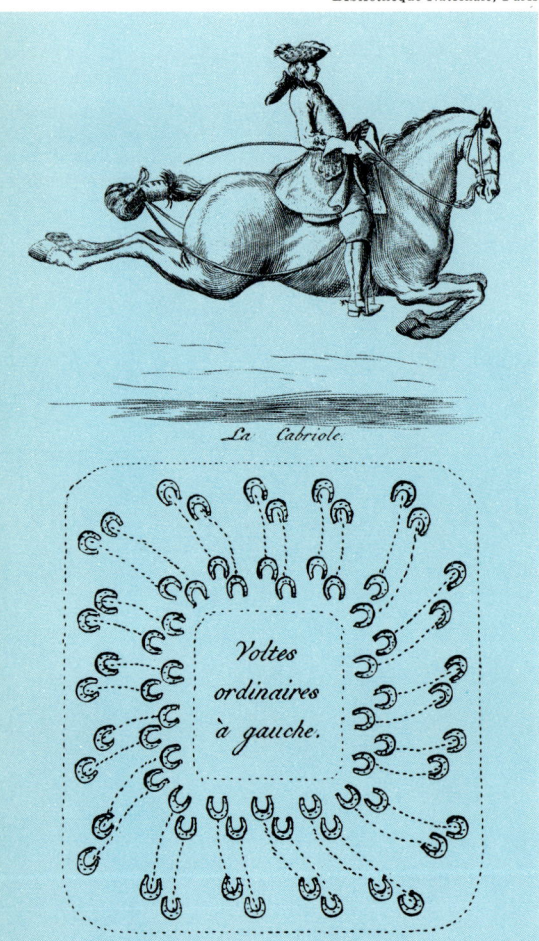

"At the end of the second act, Dupré appeared again, still wearing a mask, and danced to a different tune, but in my opinion doing exactly the same as before."

What with the complicated protocol involved with the choreographing for horses, mechanical effects, the upper and lower branches of royalty, and acrobats, matters began to get out of hand and in 1661, Louis XIV asked his ballet master, Beauchamps, to lay down some rules—to codify, classify, and name the style and all the acceptable and successfully pretty steps. To this day they are known by their 17th-century French names and that is why all ballet language is in French. The teaching of these rules constituted the founding of the Royal Academy of Dancing, the first in Europe.

In the Letters Patent for the establishment of the Academy it was stated, "The art of dancing has ever been acknowledged to be one of the most suitable and necessary arts for physical development and for affording the primary and most natural preparation for all bodily exercises, and, among others, those concerning the use of weapons, and consequently it is one of the most valuable and most useful arts for nobles and others who have the honour to enter our presence not only in time of war in our armies, but even in time of peace in our ballets."

Shortly after the Royal Academy was founded, the Opéra Ballet was established as a national theater, supported by the king. The pupils of Pécours and Beauchamps became in their turn masters and began to train the great stars who traveled from court to court throughout Europe performing and teaching, for now every king and princeling wished a royal opera and ballet, and straightway set about establishing them. And some of the smaller courts produced the most important theaters, historically speaking—notably the Ducal Theater of Württemberg at Stuttgart—because then as now young ambitious and revolutionary talents had often to leave home (the Paris Opéra) and seek recognition in less tradition-bound institutions.

In quick order the following theaters were established. In each city, ballet companies had existed without formal recognition except for large court events. But with the completion of the opera house the companies were established in permanent residence and guaranteed continuity and protection. They are all still functioning as the ornaments of the state and the repositories of great national works and technical styles.

1. The Paris Opéra—
   Founded in 1669, called for some time the Académie Royale de Musique and since 1871 known as The Théâtre Nationale de l'Opéra
2. England
   The King's Theatre—Haymarket (1705)
   Royal Opera—Covent Garden (1732)
3. The Royal Danish Ballet
   National Theater (1726)
   The Royal Theater (1748)
4. San Carlo, Naples (1737)
5. Vienna Burgtheater (1748). The old Burgtheater was used only for opera and ballet
6. Ducal Theater of Württemberg, Stuttgart (1750). The company of dancers at the time of Noverre numbered 100 with 20 soloists
7. Munich—(1752)
8. The Royal Swedish Ballet (1773)
   Founded by Gustavus III, the "Theater King"
9. Teatro alla Scala, Milan, Italy (1778)
10. Imperial Russian Ballet founded by the Czar
    Bolshoi Theater in Moscow (1776)
    Bolshoi Theater in St. Petersburg (1783) Now Maryinsky Theater (opened 1860)

Unlike all other European monarchies, England had no chartered royal ballet and school, although in the 18th century it did have a flourishing and distinguished opera. While every other capital, national or provincial, boasted a state-endowed opera house, Great Britain's music had to be self-supporting, and the opera and ballet companies were private commercial enterprises. That there were as many of them as there were gives the lie to the myth that the English are not a musical people. Since, however, there were no great schools, they had to import most of the talent. Teachers from France were continually crossing the channel and there was sufficient dance activity to entice some of the greatest choreographers to work with the London companies. The ballet productions were mounted at great cost and the ballet premieres, two or three a year, were the pride and excitement of the opera seasons.

For 100 years under private management the King's Theatre in the Haymarket produced great ballets—without, however, establishing a school, a permanent company, or a tradition.

Photo Courtesy of Lillian Moore

Bolshoi Petrovsky Theater, 1824, St. Petersburg

N. Y. Public Library Theater Collection

Haymarket Theatre, c.1825, London

Drottningholms Teatermuseum

Drottningholm Theater, Sweden. This theater is preserved in its pristine 18th-century condition because during the Napoleonic campaigns it was used as a granary. It is one of the few old theaters that did not burn.

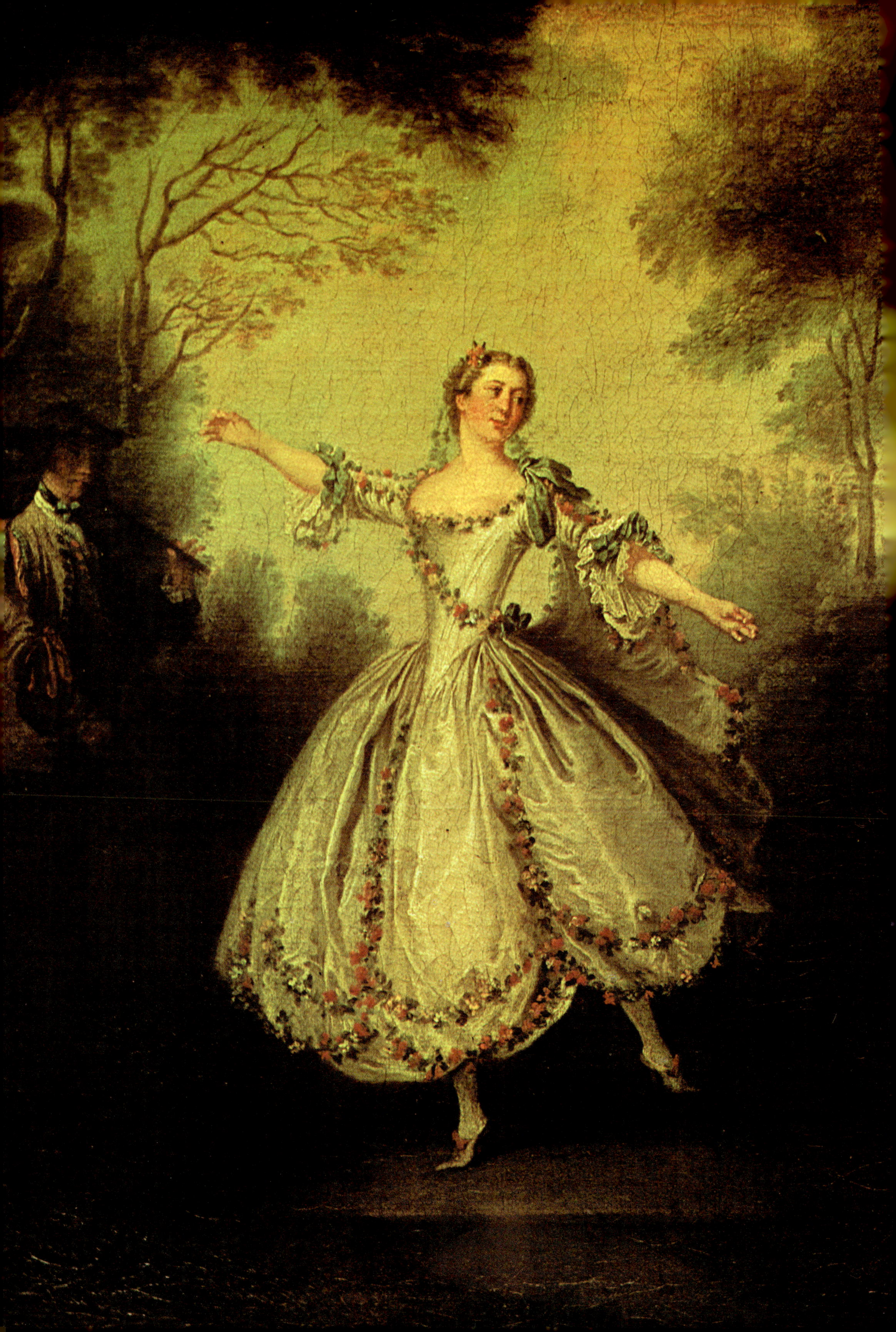

ALL the dancers throughout Europe used the same technique, devised at the head factory, the Paris Opéra.

In the two hundred and fifty years that followed, enormous expansions and enlargements have taken place, each innovation the gift of some one dancer. And so the body of technique has grown like coral.

With the development of aerial work, ballet began to become athletic, beyond even the capacities of expert swordsmen. Of all forms of dancing, ballet is the most difficult because more than any other it is preoccupied with flight, with leaving the earth. It makes aerial patterns, either by extension of the arms and legs, or by controlled jumps.

The ground is used as a base, a place to root in or to balance over, a point of departure, but never as a sounding board or as an integral part of gesture. In classic ballet there is no stamping or beating on the earth. There is no sitting down or lying. The ballet dancer never touches the floor except when kneeling, which as a courtier he was used to doing, or in moments of intense feeling such as fainting or dying. He never sat, or reclined, or fell backwards. Floors were dirty and his suit expensive. The Oriental and Polynesian do a great many dances seated. There are no seated western dances, folk or court, and consequently no seated ballet dances. This dance lives in air. This is its glory and its limitation.

Ballet is a dance for youth. Older people simply have not the stamina. In other kinds of dancing older performers can bring mature and mellow taste to the work with good effect. Not here; the lungs and the heart must be young.

But strength and exuberance are by no means all; line counts. The postures and attitudes practiced so carefully at the barre are now lifted bodily into the air.

Everything in ballet aims at giving the impression of effortless ease. Human beings are chained to the earth by gravity; but gods defied it, and kings tried to. The inheritors of their style follow suit.

The heel of the ballet foot must stretch as easily as a cat's paw. The Achilles tendon is the spring on which a dancer pushes for his jump, the hinge on which he takes the shock of landing. It springs to attention whenever it is released. It is the tension of the foot that distinguishes ballet style from other dance forms.

This alert and tense arching gives every ballet position enormous vitality. It also prolongs the line of the leg.

The ballet hand is relaxed, simple, extending the line of the arm, never affected or artificial. Any affectations of behavior are considered out of style.

Though their feet and weight must descend when gravity dictates, the slower rhythms of head and arms give the illusion of sustained flight.

Men make better jumpers than women. A second-class male soloist can usually outjump a ballerina.

*Vestris fils,
by Gainsborough*

Photo Jack Skeel A.R.P.S.
The Trustees, Adolph Hirsch Collection

The First Great Ballet Dancers

*La Carmargo by Lancret,
"Cette admirable gigotteuse, Grande Crocquese d'entrechats."*

Louis Pécour
An engraving by F. Chereau
after a painting by R. Tourniere

Collection of Lillian Moore

Charles L. Beauchamps

Bibliothèque de l'Opéra, Paris

When women jump, they jump for brilliance and quickness of footwork. Some few have great elevation, but mostly they specialize in beats rather than soaring flight.

Among the devices peculiar to ballet dancing are pirouettes or turns. These revolvings are achieved on the ball or point of the foot, on a straight knee and spine.

There are many kinds of pirouettes in all the basic positions. The multiple pirouette on one leg, sustained in balance from a single push (some great technicians can achieve 10 to 15 turns without losing balance or hopping); the chaîné or chained turns from foot to foot, very rapid and brilliant, traveling diagonally across or encircling the entire stage; the same turns, jumped or leaped with the body hanging off balance in air (but never with the axis of the spine changing or undulating during the spin).

Turns or pirouettes can be done equally well by men or women —although the supported turn is usually restricted to women, mainly for the sake of appearance.

The pantomime or story-telling part of old ballets was always separate from the dances proper and was performed in acting as artificial as sign language. This might seem stilted to us until we realize how important it is to maintain a uniform style. For example, we would not accept an ordinary colloquial conversation in the middle of grand opera. Our ears would be insulted. And so we have the recitative or sung speech and tonality is preserved. In the same way, we must have acting of a piece with the grand manner of the dance material. It is a form of acting almost as arbitrary and unrealistic as Oriental dance pantomime.

We know that all forms of emotion and tension are shown in the shoulders and neck first, with ordinary people that is—never with a ballet dancer. With a ballet dancer, the shoulders remain quiet. A ballet dancer flies into a temper or impassioned abandon with serenity.

Most of the dancers have remained anonymous and are remembered today only by their invention, a turn of the wrist, a grace and speed of foot, a lightness and brilliance of whirling; some one lovely thing representing a life's effort and bequeathed to the dancers who came after.

But a few are remembered by name.

CHARLES L. BEAUCHAMPS (1636-1705),

French dancer and choreographer who codified the classic positions and steps for Louis XIV. He specialized in pirouettes and turns in the air.

MARIE SALLÉ (1707-1756),

French dancer and choreographer of unrivaled taste, who excelled in sensitive interpretation. She made a sensation at the remarkable age of nine at Covent Garden, London, particularly because her pseudo-Greek tunics exposed her legs. Later, she created her solos in many ballets, notably *Les Indes Galantes*, at the Paris Opéra, August 23, 1735. (This ballet with choreography by Aveline, Lifar, and Lander, was revived June 18, 1952.)

Sallé was the first reformer to attempt to introduce sensible plots, sensitive interpretation, and fine characterization.

She was a moving and intelligent actress. She also reformed costumes, and by abandoning the heavy skirts and wigs of her predecessors for dresses of simple and beautiful line, which permitted free movement, she departed drastically from current practice. Her fragile muslin. tunic and her naturalness of gesture foreshadowed Isadora Duncan's innovations two centuries later.

The great choreographer J. G. Noverre wrote of her:

"She was possessed of neither the brilliancy nor the technique common to dancing nowadays, but she replaced that showiness by simple and touching graces; free from affectation, her features were refined, expressive, and intelligent. Her voluptuous dancing displayed both delicacy and lightness; she did not stir the heart by leaps and bounds."

CAMARGO (1710-1770, Marie Anne de Cupis de Camargo),

the most beloved French dancer of the 18th century. She was a great jumper, we read. And she was credited with having perfected the entrechat six or beaten jump. So that her feet could be seen, she shortened her skirts to mid-leg. Critics howled and so did moralists, but the skirts stayed up. It took 100 years to get them to the knee and another hundred to get them off.

She is supposed to have removed the heels from her slippers (although all portraits show her in heels) to help her batterie, which was brilliant. She danced with great swiftness and her jetés and pas de basque were splendid.

In his *Mémoires,* Casanova says of Camargo,

"I saw a danseuse who bounded like a fury, cutting entrechats to right and left and in all directions, but scarcely rising from the ground; yet she was received with fervent applause."

J. G. Noverre recorded the following:

"Certain writers have erred in endowing her with graces. Nature had deprived her of everything she should have had; she was neither pretty, nor tall, nor well formed; but her dancing was vivacious, light, and full of gaiety and sparkle. Jetés battus, royales, and cleanly-cut entrechats—all these steps which today have been eliminated from the vocabulary of the dance [and which in the 20th century are right back in], and which produce such a captivating effect, were executed by Mlle. Camargo with the utmost ease. She only danced to lively music, and such quick movements do not permit of the display of grace; but for this she substituted ease, speed, and gaiety, and, in a place where everything was depressing, long-drawn-out, and wearisome, it was a delight to see so animated a dancer, whose sprightliness could draw the audience from the torpor into which monotony had plunged it.

"Mlle. Camargo was intelligent and she showed it by adopting a brisk style of dancing which allowed the spectators no time to detect and catalogue her physical defects. It is a fine thing to know how to conceal one's deficiencies beneath the lustre of one's talents."

Bibliothèque de l'Opéra, Paris

Marie Sallé, after Lancret

Portrait of Marie Sallé after Fenouil

Collection of Lillian Moore

Some of her dances are preserved in contemporary graphs. Her dances were formal, elegant, impersonal, undramatic and, despite Noverre, compared to modern ballet, non-athletic.

LA BARBERINA (1721-1799, Barberina Campanini)

was an Italian dancer who specialized in pirouettes and jetés battus. She was the favorite of the court of Frederick the Great.

JEAN GEORGES NOVERRE (1727-1810),

French dancer and choreographer, called "the grandfather of the ballet"—a dancer, teacher, and choreographer, who instituted reforms that have had their full flowering only in our time. Ballets before him had been merely a collection of miscellaneous light divertissements (short dances) without relationship or dramatic reason, thrown together to any hastily assembled music. They tended to be much alike, using the same steps over and over, and were introduced at random into operas, with no regard for suitability, simply because the Parisians liked ballet. Jean Jacques Rousseau in his *Dictionary of Music* (1767) grumbled about this. So did Noverre. He insisted on:

> Unity of design, a logical and dramatic plot.
> The elimination of everything unnecessary to the central theme.
> The elimination of star turns or solos unnecessary to plot.
> Better and less old-fashioned music. A quicker and more dynamic pace.
> Simple, clear pantomime.
> New and lovely combinations of steps.
> Total reform in costume. He was opposed to the wearing of stiff clothing and masks.

He begged the dancers "to break hideous masks, to bury ridiculous perukes, to suppress clumsy panniers, to do away with still more inconvenient hip pads, to substitute taste for routine, to indicate dress more noble, more accurate, more picturesque, to demand action and expression in dancing, to demonstrate the immense distance which lies between mere mechanical technique and the genius which places dancing beside the imitative arts."

During his lifetime, he was only partially successful in getting the dancers to discard cumbersome garments. After the invention of long knitted stockings or tights (maillots) the dancers could really bare their legs and thighs and did, sometimes quite shockingly. In any case, they were able to kick and jump higher and to run more freely than ever before. At Noverre's insistence, Gaetano Vestris discarded his mask in 1770. The audience was astonished by the effect of acting on a movable face.

But Noverre's plea to all performers to turn to nature for inspiration, to use gestures that could be universally understood and not the stereotyped and artificial sign language cherished by the few, met in his time with no success. After all, he was working in the mid-eighteenth century, the age of the greatest artificialities and conceits of court life, and he was producing ballets mainly for the members of those courts.

Ehemals Staatlichen Schlosser und Garten

La Barberina by Antoine Pesne

Title page of Noverre's masterpiece

Bibliothèque de l'Opera, Paris

He had to go outside of France to the Ducal Theater in Stuttgart to make his success and to publish his great book *Lettres sur la danse* (1760). This is the classic treatise on the theory and form of dramatic dancing, and has had an incalculable influence on all who came after, but during his life Noverre never received proper recognition in Paris. His great works were performed in Stuttgart, London, and Vienna, where he collaborated with Gluck and Mozart and taught Marie Antoinette dancing. He choreographed the first performance of *Iphigénie en Tauride* in 1778. Mozart wrote *Les Petits Riens* to his scenario.

Noverre gave us the ballet d'action, or story ballet—dances arranged on a unified dramatic theme. It was on the advice of David Garrick, the English actor, that he extended the single ballet to a full evening's entertainment of five acts. Garrick called him "the Shakespeare of the dance."

None of his choreography survives even in scenario form.

GAETANO VESTRIS (1729-1808),

Italian dancer and choreographer, worked with Noverre and was able to further some of the great reformer's ideas. He was probably the first male dancer with a technique in the modern sense.

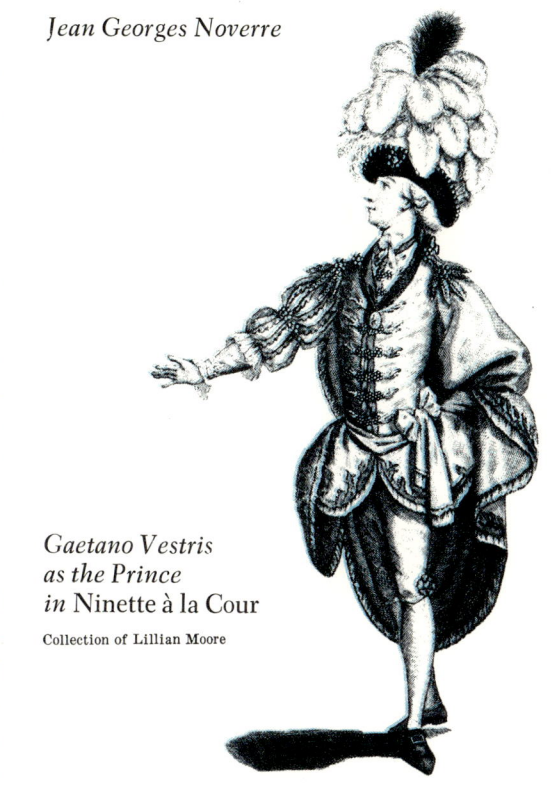

JEAN DAUBERVAL (1742-1806),

French dancer and choreographer, who did much to forward the theories of Noverre. He invented comedy ballet. His most famous work, *La Fille Mal Gardée* (1786), is presently in the repertories (at least in scenario form) of several companies, notably the Russian companies of Moscow and Leningrad (in 1882 with new choreography by Ivanov and Petipa), the American Ballet Theatre (with choreography by Nijinska), and the Royal Ballet, London (with new choreography by Frederick Ashton).

Tamara Karsavina writes in the program note to the Royal Ballet version of this work: "None of Noverre's ballets has survived to our day to bear witness to his greatness. *La Fille Mal Gardée* of his disciple Dauberval has been preserved and its pastoral fragrance has not evaporated through centuries. Perhaps the secret of its vitality may be put down to Dauberval's more spontaneous, less reasoned inspiration. While Noverre showed a marked predilection for the heroic and the tragic, Dauberval has created a first 'genre.' The tragic mode should be prevalent in the elevated art of ballet. In order to attain moral heights ballet should portray complex feelings of a noble nature, and not peasants' coarseness,' wrote Noverre. Dauberval took his inspiration from life itself, rural life at that. *La Fille Mal Gardée* is genially rustic in defiance of the artificial shepherds and shepherdesses of the pre-revolution conceptions."

In the unprecedented choice of lower class and peasant characters for heroes, *Fille* parallels that other contemporary disturbing proletarian work, Beaumarchais' *Barber of Seville*. These two dramatic pieces were the storm signals presaging the French Revolution.

Bibliothèque de l'Opéra, Paris

Jean Georges Noverre

*Gaetano Vestris
as the Prince
in* Ninette à la Cour
Collection of Lillian Moore

Jean Dauberval

Bibliothèque de l'Opéra, Paris

Marie Madeleine Guimard by Pajou

MADELEINE GUIMARD (1743-1816),

Première danseuse noble and a pupil of Noverre, a woman of reputedly little beauty but enormous charm and intellect, a splendid actress, with impeccable taste in costume and deportment. Not a great technician, but an influence for reform both in and out of the theater.

MARIE AUGUSTE VESTRIS (1760-1842),

Italian dancer, the son of Gaetano Vestris and hailed by the father as "the god of the Dance"—a superb technician, with remarkable elevation. Gaetano Vestris said of his son, Auguste, "Auguste is more skillful than I, the explanation is simple; Gaetano Vestris is his father; an advantage which Nature has denied me."

CHARLES LUDVIG DIDELOT (1767-1836),

French dancer and choreographer. He was the son of the first dancer and choreographer of the Swedish Royal Theater. He studied first with his father in Sweden, then with Dauberval, Lany, and Auguste Vestris at the Paris Opéra, making his debut there at the age of twelve. He applied many of the principles of Noverre (which he had heard discussed by Dauberval) and was successful in reforming costumes and plots.

He invented an entirely new system of teaching and ranks with the great masters of the 19th century, Blasis, Johansson, and Cecchetti. He introduced "flights"—the swinging and soaring of girls on wires. These first took to the air in his *Flore et Zéphyre* in London, 1796.

Alexander Pushkin, the great Russian poet, said there was more poetry in Didelot's ballets than in the entire French literature of the period. Didelot's works foreshadowed the romantic ballet.

Marie Auguste Vestris after Nathaniel Dance

Charles Didelot

SALVATORE VIGANÒ (1769-1821),

Italian dancer and choreographer. He was the nephew of the composer Luigi Boccherini. He studied with Dauberval in Madrid, and later became ballet master and choreographer at La Scala, Milan. Ballet in Italy had its greatest period under his influence and declined in creativity after his death.

Among his ballets were *Prometheus* (La Scala 1801) with music specially composed by Beethoven.

The ballet dancing of the 18th century was undoubtedly elegant and lovely but it would seem to us simple, not nearly so acrobatic or astonishing as what we demand today. Women were not yet up on their points. Jumps were just being devised. Lifts had not yet been attempted, nor multiple pirouettes. Tours à la séconde they had, but not the repeated turnings on a single spot called fouettés. The wild, quick whirlings about the stage, the precision of leap and turns accomplished by dozens of dancers simultaneously—all this was yet to come.

Salvatore Viganò

What, then, did the eighteenth century see? They saw what was lovely and tasteful and gracious, and for them it was enough. They had different eyes and different ears. Their senses were not assaulted all day in such a variety of disturbing and conflicting ways.

Think, for instance, of how quiet it was in the streets and houses then! A wagon wheel could be heard a quarter of a mile away, or birds or children calling. Voices were quieter. When you visualize these dances, erase from your ears all memory of motors, airplanes, horns, buzzers, telephones, or radios. A church bell or a trumpet was the loudest sound most audiences had ever heard. Sounds were simpler then and all music was simpler and purer. None who saw Camargo or Vestris had ever heard a modern symphony orchestra or even a piano. That sound was yet to come to our world—strings were still plucked, as in the harpsichord. Eyes that watched the passepied or rigaudon had never seen electric lights, arc beams, or gas lights. Eyes saw more then—stars could be watched above the streets in the greatest cities. Lamps reached far, and when one came in from the luminous dark, candlelight made all things gentle and forgiving.

Musée des Beaux Arts, Tours

Françoise Prévost in Bacchante *by Jean Raoux*

Dauberval and Marie Allard (mother of Auguste Vestris) in Sylvie.

Bibliothèque de l'Opéra, Paris

99

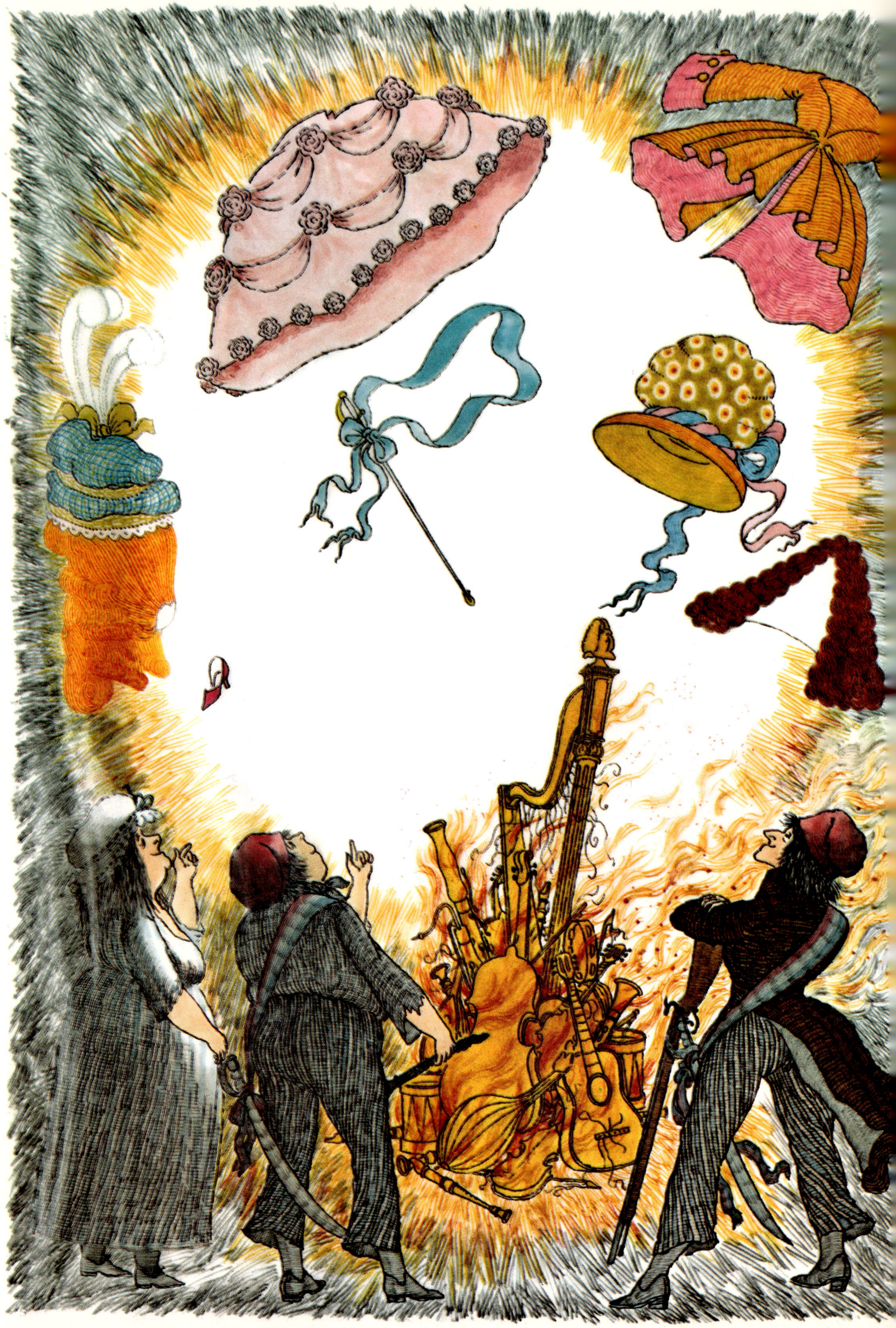

THE French Revolution put an end to these lovely pastoral scenes. The 18th century which began so graciously went out in blood and cannonades.

After the French Revolution came twenty years of Napoleonic wars with universal slaughter, and after that people did not want to hear one more word about glory.

Napoleon had altered the map of Europe, but the generals and kings who gained the field at Waterloo put it back more or less to suit themselves. They took Napoleon's family off their various thrones and installed those of their old patrons and masters who had not in the meantime got killed. On the surface matters seemed to be not too different from the Revolution.

But they were.

Very different.

The people had learned to speak out for themselves. They knew what they would never again forget: that if they wished they could change things, that it was not the will of God that they live and die in misery, silent and unprotesting. Napoleon had taught them that a common man could dominate kings if he was smart and strong.

Now they began to learn something else. They learned that sometimes by working and planning they could have money and that money was power. Not just a few of them as in the Renaissance, but many of them. This was a modern idea. For thousands of years birth or armed might had been power. Now trade or business could achieve as much. The new idea was not liked greatly by the people who had governed just by being born to the job.

But the idea was a fact.

The middle or business class had arrived. This great change was predicated on the use of steam and the invention of machinery.

A new sound was heard in the world. The sound of the mechanical loom. This was the sound of the 19th century.

The change was called the Industrial Revolution. Factories and machinery appeared, transforming the countryside and cities. Big business became an accepted way of life. The uneducated working people, the manual laborers, were as wretched as ever before, possibly more wretched. Thousands left their farms and hand looms and cottage work benches and went to the cities. And thousands died there. Slums became the lot of most workers. Poverty and crime were now herded at everyone's doorsteps, shut up in neighboring rooms. Unfortunately, the rich were no longer responsible for the poor as in feudal times; no one now was responsible. Children as well as adults died all about, next door, in the gutter before the house, at the work benches and machinery, in the mines, and in special dying houses called workhouses.

The Golden Age

Marie Taglioni (above) in Natalia, *(below) in* Le Dieu et la Bayadère, *and (opposite)* La Sylphide.

*"When I danced I smiled.
I did not laugh, I was happy."*
MARIE TAGLIONI

These things were painful to consider and people sought to escape noticing by distraction through the arts. The attempt at escape was called the Romantic movement in art. It was the protest of the individual against the sordidness and tedious cruelty of real life.

When people went to the theater these days—and many more people went than ever before—they understandably asked for things unlike what they saw around them. They asked for color, for fantasy, for delight. They asked for fairy creatures, spirits, characters from far countries, creatures anyone would like to become or dream about: gypsy girls, Italian bandits, beautiful ghosts, —anything so long as it was like nothing in everyday life. Even kings and gods could be played by the proletariat since the Revolution. The six-penny seat in the gallery was surcease, was promise, was magic, was forgetfulness.

And if the play was about kings, the kings and queens suffered romantic agonies just like any lady or gentleman, but not at all like any factory worker, housemaid, or asylum child. In the 16th- and 17th-century theater, duty always conquered love. But people had got very tired of duty; it usually led to war. They thought they would give love a trial now, and fantasy.

Victor Hugo was the leading dramatic poet of this time, and his romantic plays transformed the French theater, which had been, since Molière, Corneille, and Racine, the great theater of the western world.

The 18th-century dancer was expected to be robust, charming, and voluptuous—the 19th-century dancer was unworldly and spiritual. She was also a far greater technician.

Marie Taglioni was undoubtedly the first ballerina as we understand the term today. The professional artist had at last appeared —dedicated in childhood and cloistered throughout youth in the practice room.

The term "ballerina" is regularly misused. It does not mean any girl who takes ballet lessons. It is an exact term and its equivalent in the army is a five-star general. Below the ballerina in descending order come stars, first soloists, second soloists, coryphées, and members of the corps de ballet, or privates no grade.

"According to tradition," Anatole Chujoy explains in the spring 1959 issue of *Dance Perspectives*, "in the Russian Imperial Ballet hierarchy, a coryphée was a position between corps de ballet and soloist.... Coryphées normally danced in groups of eight or six; soloists were not required to dance in groups of more than four; ballerinas and premiers danseurs danced only pas seuls and pas de deux."

Taglioni was the greatest dancer of her century, and one of the greatest of all time. Her father was an Italian dancer and choreographer, Filippo Taglioni, and under his training, she refined every aspect of ballet technique.

With the advent of this great female star and her domination of the European opera dance, ballet as we know it came into being.

"Like a dancing flower." FANNY KEMBLE

Agnes de Mille Collection

Flower border by Elizabeth Montgomery

"In all my movements, I remained straight, without strain; you could not hear me descend, because it was always my toe which struck first, the heel following gently on the ground. I adored all those steps in which I experienced an elevation which kept me almost from feeling the earth. Literally, I vibrated in the air." MARIE TAGLIONI

FILIPPO TAGLIONI (1778-1871),

Italian dancer and choreographer, made his debut at Pisa in 1794, later studied under Coulon and made his French debut at the Opéra.

He did not invent the new balletic style; he perfected, developed, and advertised it on Marie's body. She was not his only child. He sired a dynasty. His son, Paul, married a German ballerina, Amalia Galster, and their children carried the great tradition all over Europe and America and perpetuated the style for fifty years.

The pallid and sugary scores of Taglioni's ballets, most of which were choreographed for his daughter, have been discarded; the ballets are lost. The influence of his style remains.

MARIE TAGLIONI (1804-1884)

was her father's chief apostle. She seemed all gauze and air and she had perfected the lovely trick of dancing on the ends of her toes. She was a great jumper, not in the brisk lively sense that Camargo had been, but as we know jumpers today—soaring, commanding, winged. All the critics speak of her enormous stride and her long horizontal leaps or jetés; she could cross the Paris Opéra stage in three bounds. She could lift herself into the air and float with greater loveliness than any woman in recorded history. Her personal style on stage was so exquisite that she changed the entire aspect of her art forever.

Her father swore that no one had ever heard her foot fall and that if anyone ever did he would disown her.

In order to dance on point the arch had to be developed to support the weight of the body. This involved a new technique for the foot and a tremendous strengthening of the ankle, knee, and back.

Taglioni and her contemporaries wore slippers without stiffening, as fragile as silk gloves, made of light strips of silk ribbon and weighing six ounces, as frail as a piece of cardboard. She had support only from the darning of the toes and the binding of the ribbons around her ankles, and could therefore only mount to her toes for poses, and take a few short steps on point. The sustained traveling steps and grinding pirouettes done today were not possible for the first point dancers.

Taglioni had a new pair of slippers for every act of her ballets. The stage of the opera house was purposely dirty to prevent slipping. Today, for the same reason, the floor is either wet lightly with a watering pot, or dusted with rosin. Every stage has a rosin box in the corner. Slipping is the dancer's nightmare.

She dropped all weighty costumes because she was really dancing, riding, striding the air, beating her legs like humming bird wings, lighting and balancing on the very tips of her toes. She discarded also the too revealing and often immodest tunic of the Empire period. In its place she had Lami design for her a special skirt of gauze that has become the standard ballet uniform. She parted her hair straight in the center and kept the curls and bun tight to her head; this also has become traditional. Her arms were ungainly and long. Her father taught her to cross her arms on her breast, or hold them low with crossed wrists to keep them out of the way. This attempt to conceal what her teacher considered a defect influenced balletic style for the next seventy years. Dr. L. Véron, director of the Paris Opéra, wrote, "...Poor Marie Taglioni became the butt for the mockery of her companions. 'Will that little hunch-back,' said one, 'ever learn to dance?'"

But Marie Taglioni's contribution went beyond elevation and toe dancing, beyond personal style. She changed the performer's point of view and with it, of course, the audience's. She demonstrated that dancing could express something more than mere sensuous delight. Her quality was predominantly chaste and spiritual. Her father boasted that any gentleman could bring his wife to see her without blushing. The Czar, unable to believe that her knees would remain invisible in her great soaring leaps, left the Imperial Box and went down into the stalls to see. Even from this vantage, she appeared modest and exquisite, her knees mysteriously not on view!

She took all Europe by storm with her "indescribable mixture of artlessness and boldness." "She was," said Fanny Kemble, "like a dancing flower." Wherever she went new ballet styles and techniques sprang up, even in the far and savage Russias.

With this caliber of performer came the professional critic and the informed audience.

Everyone wanted to make a hit in Paris because that was where the great dance audiences were and the most powerful critics, chiefly the novelist Théophile Gautier, who collaborated on the scenario of *Giselle*. With his words, and those of his newspaper friends, we have for the first time in the history of dancing contemporary critical descriptions by writers who are concerned with individual technique and performing style and who are trained to observe the differences.

There is much more material on the women than on the men because male dancers were despised, and while the critics were condescending even to the females, they found them attractive. They wrote as though they were making love to the ladies, which in the case of Gautier could not be proved untrue. This approach is no longer thought to be in good taste. Critics today are not supposed to be in love with their subjects; it is not considered sporting.

"Taglioni floats like a blush of light before our eyes," wrote *The Monthly Chronicle* in 1838. "We cannot perceive the subtle means by which she contrives, as it were, to disdain the earth, and to deliberate her charming motions in the air.... She achieves the office of wings without their encumbrance. Her sweetness and gentleness have a wooing tone, which breathes from her with no more external appearance than the aroma from flowers..."

"Taglioni alone *finishes* the step or the pirouette, or the arrowy bound over the scene, as calmly, as accurately, as faultlessly as she begins it. She floats out of a pirouette as if, instead of being made giddy, she had been lulled by it into a smiling and childlike dream, and instead of tiring herself and her aplomb (as is seen in all other dancers, by their effort to recover composure), it had been the moment when she had rallied and been refreshed. The smile, so expressive of enjoyment in her own grace, which steals over Taglioni's lips when she does a difficult step, seems communicated

Agnes de Mille Collection

"My hands and feet were spiritual."

Agnes de Mille Collection

in an indefinable languor to her limbs. You cannot fancy her fatigued when, with her peculiar softness of motion, she courtesies to the applause of an enchanted audience, and walks lightly away..."

N. P. WILLIS
Famous Persons and Famous Places

"She was not beautiful, her figure was a little flat, her arms were long. To see her appear for the first time, at rest, she inspired a deep feeling of sympathy; her modest demeanour, her downcast eyes, her gentle, open expression, proclaimed an amiable person having the wish to please without any pretensions, one of those rare characters with no harshness in her nature. All this is true as regards the woman.

"But the dancer!

"She began, she raised those arms which worried us, they were two garlands; she smiled, she seemed happy; she was a child leaping in time, as if she had not a care in the world, executing as she played tours de force which became miracles of grace. In three bounds she traversed the stage from one end to the other; she flew, she never touched the ground; her breathing remained untroubled; her feet, real jewels, appeared as much at home in their satin slippers as those of a pretty farm-girl in her little wooden shoes. And then, when this prodigious flight was ended, she came to the front of the stage, and took up her usual pose, without any grimaces and without any apparent effort.

"Taglioni invested her being with a simplicity, even an artlessness, which eliminated every suggestion of labour and difficulty; to see her thus you might imagine that you could do the same things without any difficulty, and that she was only there to amuse herself.

"She it was who first revealed to us the danse ballonnée, her skirt almost flew above her head and yet she seemed the personification of modesty. She must be seen to be believed. Others have unsuccessfully sought to equal her without reaching to the height of that slender and well-attached ankle which accorded such distinction to her steps. Her legs were finely-shaped. As for her feet, Victor Hugo has recorded their qualities far better than I could hope to do by autographing a book he sent her:

'A vos pieds—à vos ailes.'"

JACQUES RAYNAUD
Portraits Contemporains

Gautier wrote of Taglioni: "When she appears on the stage you always see the white mist bathed in transparent muslin, the ethereal and chaste vision, the divine delight which we know so well. Fortunate woman! Always the same elegant and slender form, the same calm, intelligent, and modest features. What airiness! Her tireless feet could run over blades of grass without bending them." He returns to reality on occasion: "The new style led to a great abuse of white gauze, tulle, and tarlatan; white was the only color used." (Today these romantic ballets are known as "white ballets.")

Sacheverell Sitwell says, "She had the mysterious faculty of appearing to remain quite still in the air at the apex of her flight, and then to come down slowly in defiance of the laws of gravity, an illusionary gift or secret which has only been shared with her by Vestris, and later Nijinsky, and which from remarks let drop both by Taglioni and Nijinsky is a method of breathing."

Taglioni with her *Sylphide* (1832) ushered in what became known as the Golden Age of Ballet; there appeared simultaneously and victoriously a galaxy of brilliant stars.

Ballet stars and choreographers visited all about, from opera house to opera house, the choreographers restaging their hits often under new titles, the stars performing their special roles. They were in tremendous demand, frequently more famous and better paid than singers. No contemporary diva could match Taglioni's box-office draw.

It will be noticed that the great ballet companies of the 18th and 19th centuries were state supported and that the personnel of the troupes remained permanent. The dancers were accepted into the schools as children, as many boys as girls, were trained in dancing, languages, and letters, were exhibited in the state theaters, and were later retired and given a life-pension, like any deserving civil servants. Dancers intermarried, and the great historic performers were dynastic, rearing and training their children to stardom.

A number of fine teachers worked in Italy and France contemporaneously.

CARLO BLASIS (1797-1878),

choreographer and maître de ballet at La Scala, laid down the definitive analysis of ballet.

"Before the advent of the celebrated Carlo Blasis," writes Tamara Karsavina, "the teaching of our art based itself on an intuitive search. In all justice he should be called the first pedagogue of our art. The starting point of his theory being that the immutable laws of equilibrium applied to the human body necessitated the finding of a precise formula determining the perfect balance of a dancer.... To elucidate his formula to his pupils Carlo Blasis drew geometrical schemes, in which the correlation of the different parts of the body was expressed by planimetric terminology—curves and right angles. When a pupil had assimilated the lineal structure of the dance, Blasis passed on to rounding the positions, giving them a plastic perfection."

He taught for the greater part of his life in Milan, and pupils flocked from all over the world to study with him. He taught most of the very great dancers of the last century and most of the great teachers, including Lepri who taught Cecchetti who taught the current generation of masters. So we have a straight unbroken tradition of Italian style as a foundation for all our different variations of technique.

In 1820, when he was 23, Blasis published his *Treatise on the Dance,* which has been the foundation of all subsequent training, and any changes since have been merely embellishments and superficial deviations. The basics stand. Balletic line today is virtually what it was in 1820. The practice exercises on the whole are identical although not performed in the same sequence. The ballet students strive for the same visual effects, the same points of control, the same strengths and dynamics.

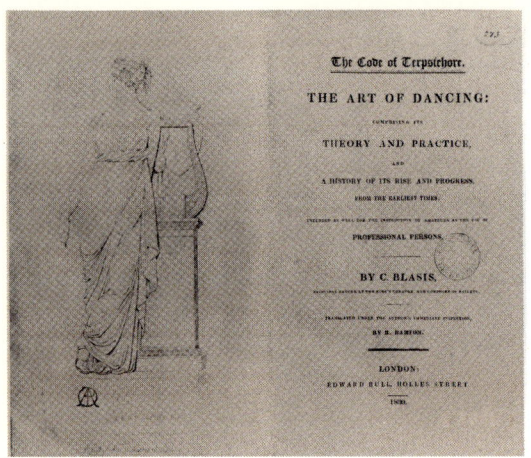

The code of practice is identical the world over. It always begins with deep knee bends and the stretching of the feet and thighs according to rules laid down by Carlo Blasis. But certain national characteristics, due partially to the physical differences of the dancers as well as divergent taste, became apparent during the 19th century. The Italians stressed brilliance and neatness of footwork, and brilliance of pirouettes, but they neglected jumps. Both French and Italians were rigidly meticulous about arm movements and allowed no freedom there. The Danes were somewhat more romantic and free and developed acting techniques. On their part, the Russians were more vigorous, freed the entire body line, the spine, arms, and head. Their kicks and extensions grew higher.

By the "Golden Forties," ballet technique was crystallized, although there was much yet to be developed—virtuoso pointwork, for example, made possible by the stiffening shoe, acrobatic lifts, and realistic acting. The 19th-century style was milder, more circumspect and controlled than what we see today. The accent was on lightness and impeccably fleet footwork.

Title page and drawings from
The Art of Dancing *by Carlo Blasis.*

FANNY ELSSLER (1810-1884),

a Viennese, was the daughter of Joseph Haydn's copyist. She was a great beauty and a superb technician, and she resembled the 18th-century dancers in their voluptuous appeal. This was not surprising since she had trained with the 18th-century star and teacher, Auguste Vestris. She became famous for her Andalusian and European folk dances as well as for her brilliant point work. She set the style, later followed by nearly all ballerinas, of including fancy versions of folk dances in repertory.

She was not a jumper like Taglioni, but a dancer terre à terre, brilliant, taquetée, with a style consisting of quick steps, precise, close together, and digging into the stage. Her points were marvelous, the beauty of her arms and hands unequaled. Gautier says: "She is the dancer for men as Mlle. Taglioni was the dancer for women." (Taglioni was neither dead, nor retired; she was dancing at this time in Russia and the use of the past tense represents a typically Parisian reproach for paying attention to any city but the French capital.) "Elssler has elegance, beauty, a bold and petulant vigor, a sparkling smile, an air of Spanish vivacity tempered by her German artlessness. Mlle. Taglioni is a Christian dancer.... Fanny is a quite pagan dancer.... She dances with the whole of her body, from the crown of her head to the tips of her toes.... It is not the aerial and virginal grace of Taglioni, it is something more human, more appealing to the senses.... At the tips of her rosy fingers ["too heavily rouged," said the English critic Chorley] quiver ebony castanets; now she darts forward, the castanets begin their sonorous chatter. With her hands she seems to shake down great clusters of rhythm. How she twists! How she bends! What fire! What voluptuousness! What precision! Her swooning arms toss about her drooping head, her body curves backward, her white shoulders seem almost to graze the ground."

It was said by less enraptured critics that Elssler's Spanish dances were pallid beside the originals, but they were the only Spanish steps most of her audiences had ever seen. She ravished Paris. Chorley wrote: "If Mme. Taglioni flew, she [Elssler] flashed. The one floated onto the stage like a nymph, the other showered every sparkling fascination around her like a sorceress." Jules Janin commented: "Elssler's steps are so finished, her dancing so correct, her feet so agile that one wonders whether she really dances or is standing still."

All of this means, in simple language, that Taglioni was one of the lightest and most aerial dancers that ever trod the stage, that her manner was quiet and restrained, and that she was a limited actress. Elssler, on the other hand, had a supple back and brilliant feet, danced with enormous rhythm and verve, was a past mistress of dynamics, and used every trick of personality and coquetry at her disposal. She obviously could not jump and never tried to except once when, with disastrous results, she attempted to follow Taglioni in the role of "Sylphide."

All the critics spoke of Elssler's acting powers. Gautier says flatly: "As a mime she is unrivaled."

Collection of Lillian Moore

*Fanny Elssler in her
New York dressing room
An engraving by Kohler
after a painting by H. Inman*

Casts of Elssler's hand and foot

Photo Courtesy of Lillian Moore

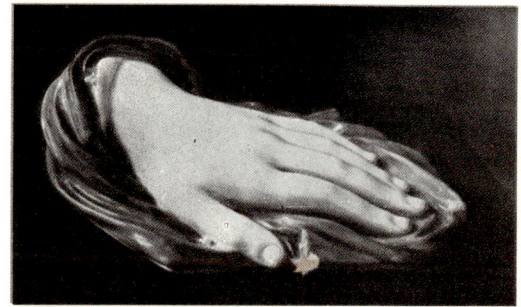

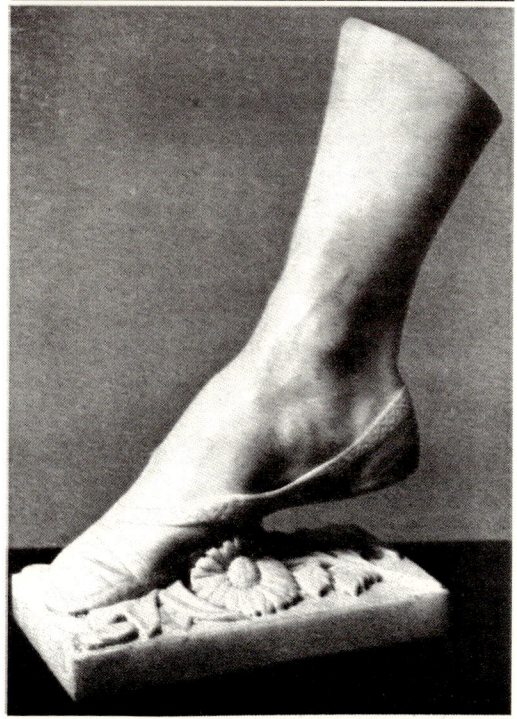

Photo Courtesy of Lillian Moore

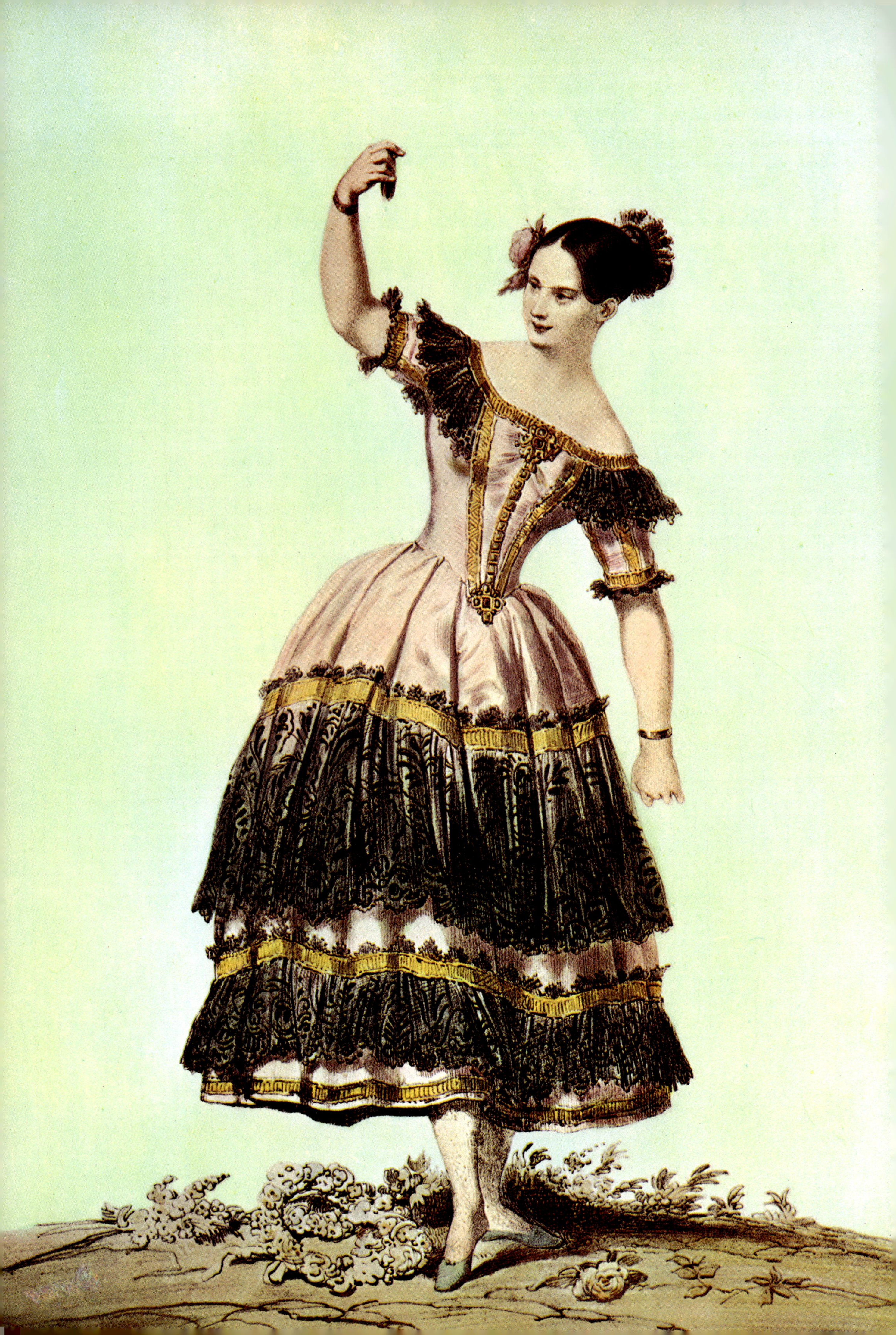

Fanny Elssler in the Cachucha from Le Diable Boiteux

FANNY CERRITO (1817-1909)

was second only to Marie Taglioni in international reputation. She was married to the choreographer St.-Léon. According to contemporaries, she was "bondante et abondante," bounding and abounding, vivacious and voluptuous, with great strengths and brio, or technical excitement. She resembled in her style somewhat the young American Augusta Maywood. She was a choreographer as well as dancer.

"She is fair," wrote Gautier. "Her blue eyes have both brilliance and tenderness; her leg is slender and she has a pretty foot. Her principal qualities are grace of pose, unusual attitudes, quickness of movement, and the rapidity with which she covers the ground ... her arms, that bugbear of most dancers, float softly in the air like pink draperies. She radiates a sense of happiness, brilliance and smiling ease which knows neither labor nor weariness."

CARLOTTA GRISI (1819-1899),

an Italian dancer for whom the ballet *Giselle* was created, dominated the ballet scene of four countries for more than a decade. Her teacher and husband was the great dancer and choreographer, Jules Perrot (1810-1892), and he was responsible for launching her career.

Of her Gautier wrote, "She exceeds all expectations in pantomime, not a single conventional gesture. Carlotta became his [Perrot's] favorite pupil; to her natural gifts he joined those that may be acquired by art; to grace he added strength, to vivacity precision, to intrepidity sureness, and, more than all these, that rhythmic harmony of movement, that finish in small details, that elegance, that beauty of pose of which he alone possesses the secret." Henry F. Chorley, in *Thirty Years' Musical Recollections,* added "...she looked shy and young and delicate and fresh. There was something of the briar rose in her beauty."

LUCILE GRAHN (1819-1907),

born in Denmark, "the Taglioni of the North," had "melancholy grace, dreamy abandon, nonchalant lightness, a Valkyrie walking on the snow," wrote Gautier. She excelled in pirouettes taught her by her teacher and choreographer, August Bournonville (1805-1879). She created his version of *Giselle* in Denmark and his version of *La Sylphide.* These are the ones currently performed. Later, she choreographed for Wagner in Bayreuth.

AUGUSTA MAYWOOD (1825- ?),

an American dancer who, after a brilliant start in Philadelphia and New York, went to Paris and studied at the Opéra under Mazilier and Coralli, making her debut there at the age of fifteen. She was an immediate hit and went on from glory to glory, being compared to and ranked with Elssler, Cerrito, Grahn, and Grisi, even in their own great roles. Important works were created for

Lucille Grahn in Eoline, ou la Dryade

Portrait bust of Fanny Cerrito by P. Gayrard

Carlotta Grisi in Giselle

Augusta Maywood, 1853, lithograph by Pieroni

her. She performed as ballerina in most of the European opera houses, partnered by the greatest men, but settled at last in Italy, starring at La Scala for years and touring the country with her own splendid little troupe, the first traveling ballet company. She never returned to America. Her fame was entirely European.

Her technique was apparently prodigious; her jumps, entrechats, and pirouettes compared to those of male stars like Perrot. She was vivacious and, like nearly all Americans, an excellent actress.

"Abrupt, unexpected, bizarre . . . sinews of steel, joints of a jaguar, and an agility approaching that of clowns. . . . In two or three bounds, she cleared this great theatre from backdrop to prompter's box, making those almost horizontal bal penchés which made the fame of Perrot the Aeriel; and then she began to gambol, to turn in the air against herself. You would have said a rubber ball bouncing on a racquet she has such elevation and spring; her little legs of a wild doe make steps as long as those of Mlle. Taglioni," wrote Gautier in 1839.

These brilliant stars gave a luster to the thirties, forties, and fifties of the last century that was not to be approached again for sixty years.

Four of them were brought together in one performance for Queen Victoria in 1845 in which Jules Perrot, the choreographer, succeeded in doing the impossible; satisfying all four ladies and the Queen besides.

These women shaped balletic style because it was for these women that the great choreographers, often their partners, created the influential works.

Collection of Parmenia Migel Ekstrom

Below: Carlotta Grisi, Marie Taglioni, Lucille Grahn, and Fanny Cerrito in the Pas de Quatre, *1845. Note that Taglioni's only true rival, Elssler, was absent from the quartet. Marie explained "We owe the beginning of bad taste to the Elssler sisters . . . their joint efforts produced considerable effect; but one could not call this art."*
Right: a modern version reconstructed by Anton Dolin. The dancers are Violette Verdy, Alicia Markova, Lupe Serrano, and Ruth Ann Koesun.

From Cyril Beaumont. "The Complete Book of Ballet." Putnam. London, 1949.

Fred Fehl

The great male dancers and choreographers of the mid-century were (besides Filippo Taglioni and his son, Paul):

JEAN CORALLI (1779-1854),

Paris-born, Italian-French dancer and choreographer, studied at the Opéra and made his debut in 1802. He later choreographed in Vienna, Milan, Lisbon, and Paris. He created *Giselle*, which is in nearly every repertory today.

JOSEPH MAZILIER (1797-1868),

French dancer and choreographer, partnered Marie Taglioni in *La Sylphide*, danced with all the stars at the Opéra. He choreographed many ballets but none of his works are now performed. They have all been lost.

Musée des Arts Décoratifs, Paris

Taglioni and her brother Paul in La Sylphide

JULES PERROT (1810-1892),

French dancer and choreographer, began his career as a circus pantomimist, later studied at the Opéra under Viganò and Auguste Vestris. He was short and ugly. Vestris told him to keep moving all the time so that the audience would not have a chance to look at his face. In spite of this, however, Gautier remarks: "Before he had made a single step it was not difficult to recognize the quiet agility, the perfect rhythm, and the easy grace of the dancer's miming." He became known for his great elevation and bounding strength. "Perrot the airy, Perrot the sylph, Perrot the male Taglioni! . . . Perrot is visible music . . . the greatest dancer in the world," wrote Gautier. Marie Taglioni, who wished all the glory, refused to continue dancing with him. The jealousy of entrenched directors blocked his career as well. He had expected to create *Giselle* for his wife, Carlotta Grisi, but the work was taken out of his hands by Coralli, chief choreographer at the Opéra, and although Perrot staged most of her solo passages, he received scant recognition and could make no headway in Paris. He exiled himself to London and produced brilliant works there for over a decade. He danced and choreographed everywhere in Europe, restaging his works at all the great opera houses. But he wished top spot at the top house; that is, he longed to be choreographer-in-chief at the Paris Opéra. This position he was only able to hold briefly, and he died a bitter and disappointed man.

From his circus days, he had evolved ideas of rhythmic pantomime and technique of simple but telling stage situation. Noverre's traditions, as realized by his pupils Didelot and Dauberval, became an organic element in the creative power of Perrot.

Of his many excellent works none have been performed recently except *Esmeralda,* created for Grisi but interpreted subsequently by all the 19th-century ballerinas in Russia.

Bibliothèque de l'Opéra, Paris

Jules Perrot

The choreography of Bournonville is preserved to this day. Portrayed are Flemming Flindt and Margrethe Schanne. Above right: Lucille Grahn and Bournonville in La Sylphide, *1836*

AUGUST BOURNONVILLE (1805-1879),

Danish dancer and choreographer, a pupil of his father, Antoine Bournonville, and of Galeotti. He studied at the Royal Danish Ballet School and made his debut at the Royal Opera in Copenhagen in 1813. He later studied in Paris.

He partnered all the great in his youth, but gave up dancing to devote himself to choreography. His works constitute the backbone of the Danish repertory. It was through him that the ideas of his father's teacher, Noverre, first found full development. He introduced, and made popular, unity of mime and style, fine pantomime, virile dancing for men, and the flowing, lyric composition of all pieces.

His style was strongly rooted in the lyric French school of Auguste Vestris and it is Vestris' style that we see now in the

August Bournonville by Bloch

Danish classic repertory. The dances are exquisitely composed and freer in form and feeling than the later Russian or Petipa School. The pantomime is also less stilted. His imprint on the Danish style was decisive and the schooling and character of performance has changed little since. He was a master teacher, and several of his pupils carried his theories abroad: Lucile Grahn, wherever she danced and in her choreography for Wagner at Bayreuth, and Christian Johansson, as a dancer and teacher at St. Petersburg.

The Danes have maintained their style, the Bournonville-Vestris style, with less disintegration and corruption than any other national company. A century later it is still intact. The Danes were less influenced by Diaghileff than any other European company and did not modify their manner in any way until Fokine visited them in 1925 and taught them the manner in which to perform his works.

The Danish dancers are careful of the works entrusted to them and never fall into the lapses of exaggeration, bad taste, or frivolity seen in other companies.

As with most state theaters, the older members become teachers and pantomimists and their acting is of a specially high order. When we see the Bournonville ballets today we are watching very nearly what he himself saw, and what is most wonderful, we are watching in large measure what Auguste Vestris saw. This is rare, almost unique in the history of dancing, certainly in the Occident.

ARTHUR ST.-LÉON (1821-1870),

French dancer and choreographer. Studying under his father, the ballet master at Stuttgart, he made his debut at the age of fourteen in Munich playing the violin. He was not an outstanding dancer, say some, with round shoulders and stooping figure, but Gautier spoke of his "fearless vigor and the ease with which he rose in the air." He partnered many, but chiefly Fanny Cerrito whom he married. He danced at the Paris Opéra (1847-1852) and was Maître de Ballet there (1863-1870).

His ambition and egomania were notorious and he considered himself unsurpassed as a choreographer. He tried to keep down rivals and succeeded rather too often. He remained throughout his life extremely jealous, could not stand criticism, and never commanded the love or respect of his colleagues.

His output, however, was large and successful. He traveled about Europe staging his ballets, often under different titles and presumably for the fees due new original pieces. His best known work is *Coppélia,* still played in many versions.

LUCIEN PETIPA (1815-1898),

French dancer and choreographer. Studied under his father, Jean, at Brussels where his father was Maître de Ballet. Debut at Paris Opéra, 1840, partnering Elssler in *La Sylphide*. Created Albrecht in *Giselle* and leads in *La Jolie Fille de Gand, La Péri* (with Grisi). He was later Maître de Ballet at the Paris Opéra, 1865.

Bibliothèque de l'Arsenal, Paris

Arthur St.-Léon

Carlotta Grisi and Lucien Petipa in La Péri, *1843*

Harvard Theatre Collection

Marius Petipa

Marius Petipa in La Fille de Pharaon

From V. Svetlov. "Le Ballet Contemporain." de Brunhoff, Editeur. Paris, 1912.

MARIUS PETIPA (1822-1910),

studied under his father Jean Petipa, made his debut at Nantes, France, and Parisian debut at the Opéra opposite Elssler, in 1841 in *Le Diable Boiteux*. He was an excellent partner, a very good actor and mime. His stage deportment became an example for generations of ballet dancers. His partnering of Grisi in *La Péri* was spoken of for generations, particularly the way he caught her in a jump from a high platform: "A pas which will soon be as famous as the Niagara Falls," said Gautier. In other words it was what we would call a "high fish," apparently attempted here for the first time.

He was graceful, passionate, and touching, and without being the prodigious technician that Perrot was, proved to be perhaps the finest partner of the century. He was gallant and modest and never tried to draw attention from the lady to himself, but danced solely for her, a trait which endeared him to female stars.

He went to St. Petersburg in 1847 and became Maître there in 1862, succeeding the veteran Jules Perrot.

Marius Petipa formed the style of the full-length ballet in four or five acts, still popular in Russia. His ballets were a combination of virtuoso pieces and spectacles. They were always the vehicle for a ballerina. His pas de deux have rarely been equaled since, possibly only by George Balanchine, Frederick Ashton, and Roland Petit. His style was a blend of French Plastique and the Italian Allegro. He explored the classic technique to its limits and became the acknowledged founder of the present Russian school of balletic movement.

He was a master at stage effects and if his ballets are all built on the same scheme, they always work. He incorporated many folk dances into his scenes. They are invariably, however, danced in balletic style.

Tchaikovsky composed to his order. Petipa dictated the forms and styles desired, the length, tempo, and beat. This tended to be regular with no sudden changes in time, a formula which Debussy and Stravinsky were to alter drastically.

Petipa counted out consistently in groups of eight, and the patterns were always three repeats of the same technical trick and a fourth variant to finish; they are, however, still delightful to watch. He established the pas de deux or duet pattern, a compact suite consisting of a duo, the woman's solo, the man's solo, and a brilliant fast duet to top all. Dancers from all over Europe flocked to study with him and to star in the works he devised for them.

He was meticulous in his preparations, doing exhaustive research and preparing minute plans for painters and composers. He always considered, however, that the choreography should take precedence over the music, decor, and libretto.

In fifty years at St. Petersburg, he created 60 full-length ballets and innumerable short ballets and dance numbers.

The spell that ballet cast in the 19th century was not due to the dancing alone, but partly also to the great spectacle it provided.

From Cyril Beaumont, "The Complete Book of Ballet."
Putnam. London, 1949.

Grisi's famous jump into the arms of Lucien Petipa in La Péri, *1843.*

A direct inheritance from the court ballets were the armies of dancers, the ranks of lovely young girls moving alike or marching in formation, the scenes, vistas, visions, and transformations. Sprites and nymphs flew through the air or skimmed over the water, and devils disappeared into the earth or into flame. Giselle was disclosed sitting on the branch of a tree (as in the current Bolshoi revival); at dawn she literally melted into the grave and grass and flowers enfolded her. Grottos turned into palaces before dazzled audiences, or into magic gardens. This was all the more wonderful when we realize that the lighting was still gas or lime. The machinery of every opera house was intricate; the floors were beautifully devised to rise, lower, or turn around, and the fly galleries and cat-walks were miracles of ingenuity. Some of the wonderful machines date back to the 18th century and are still perfectly usable.

The rapid and gorgeous changes of scenes were possible because none of the scenery was built solidly (as is often the custom now), but painted on flat canvas and cut out and pasted to nets. These could be "flown" instantly overhead. Each ballet had acres of painted scenery.

The wooden machinery beneath the stage which produced the transformations is still intact in the Drottningholm Theater in Stockholm.

Drottningholms Teatermuseum

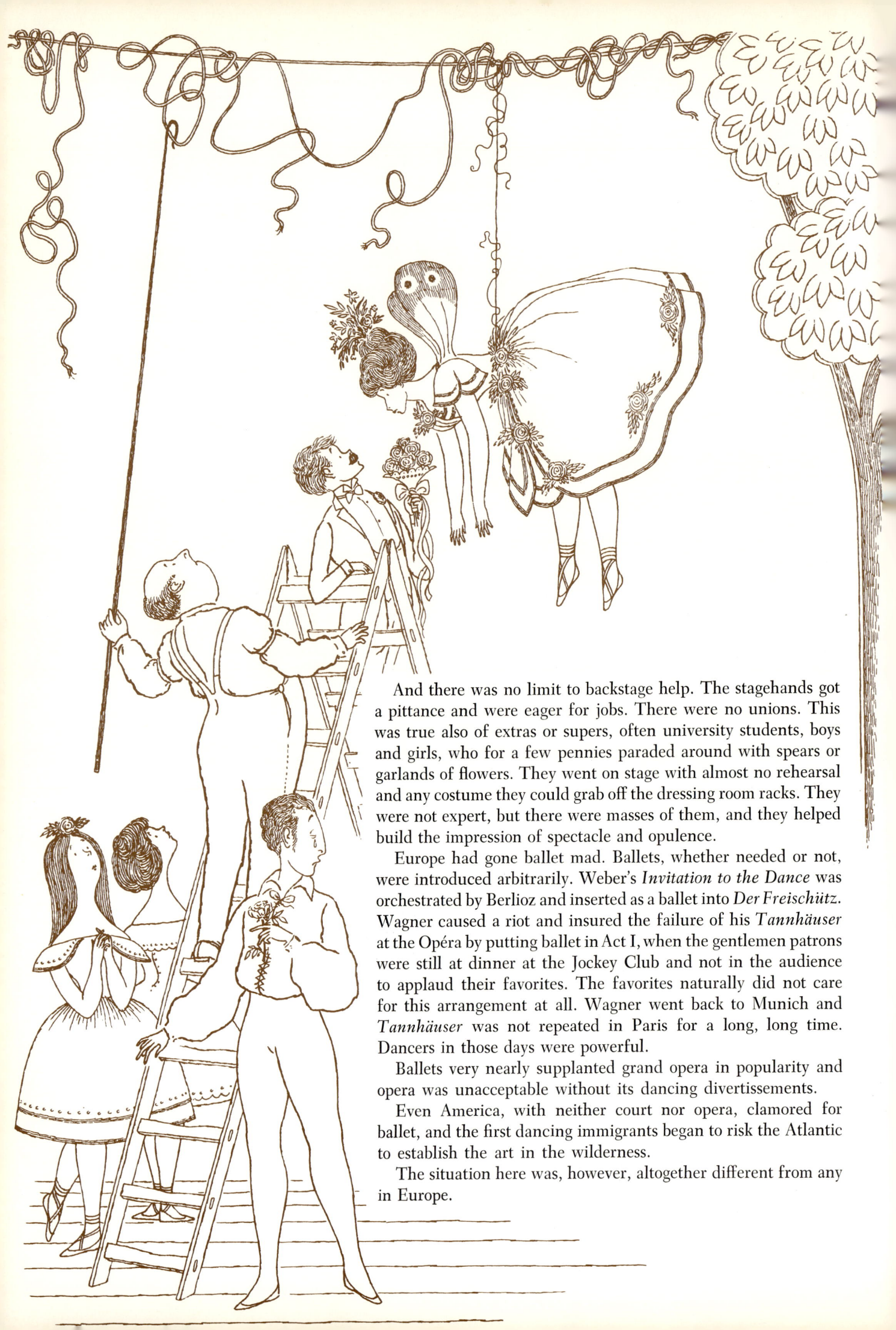

And there was no limit to backstage help. The stagehands got a pittance and were eager for jobs. There were no unions. This was true also of extras or supers, often university students, boys and girls, who for a few pennies paraded around with spears or garlands of flowers. They went on stage with almost no rehearsal and any costume they could grab off the dressing room racks. They were not expert, but there were masses of them, and they helped build the impression of spectacle and opulence.

Europe had gone ballet mad. Ballets, whether needed or not, were introduced arbitrarily. Weber's *Invitation to the Dance* was orchestrated by Berlioz and inserted as a ballet into *Der Freischütz*. Wagner caused a riot and insured the failure of his *Tannhäuser* at the Opéra by putting ballet in Act I, when the gentlemen patrons were still at dinner at the Jockey Club and not in the audience to applaud their favorites. The favorites naturally did not care for this arrangement at all. Wagner went back to Munich and *Tannhäuser* was not repeated in Paris for a long, long time. Dancers in those days were powerful.

Ballets very nearly supplanted grand opera in popularity and opera was unacceptable without its dancing divertissements.

Even America, with neither court nor opera, clamored for ballet, and the first dancing immigrants began to risk the Atlantic to establish the art in the wilderness.

The situation here was, however, altogether different from any in Europe.

I<small>N</small> America we find something unusual in the history of civilized countries: little theater and no official support of any kind. This situation had prevailed hitherto only in Moslem countries. On this point Islam and Puritanism saw eye to eye.

In the 17th century there had been no theater at all and practically no music except hymns. The people were kept busy enough just staying alive. Besides, their religion forbad frivolous pleasure, particularly theater. This was most especially true of New England. Even social dancing was rigorously restricted. Increase Mather's *An Arrow against Profane and Promiscuous Dancing, drawne out of the Quiver of the Scriptures* ("promiscuous" is taken to mean dancing between men and women) condemned only dancing that aroused the passions. But the church fathers had long ago found that just holding hands did that, and what the Puritan preachers thought permissible for boys and girls would not be considered much fun. All theater was a trap of the devil or "old ugly," as he was called.

Furthermore, theater presupposes not only leisure but congregations of people. For the most part our communities were sparse and scattered.

What diversions there were were fairly savage: ducking, flogging, pillorying, riding out of town tarred and feathered, or listening to hair-raising sermons on the tortures of hell. There was also witchcraft (as there so often is where there is no proper entertainment) and the trying and hanging of wizards and witches.

With the growth of cities during the 18th century, troupes of English players began to arrive, performing in New York and Philadelphia and Alexandria, and even, most daringly, in Boston. George Washington was a great theater-goer. Finally, there arrived a troupe of ballet dancers and wire-walkers, with one good French choreographer. But they had to work with untrained native talent for chorus.

The best dancers, however, stayed in Europe. A trip across the Atlantic in those days was perilous and lengthy and in colonial America the financial rewards for performers were negligible.

During the American Revolution the prejudice against English performers was understandably acute and lasted until well after the War of 1812.

At the end of the 18th century the leading gentlemen of our thirteen states wrote the American constitution. It was the best constitution to date in the world, and provided for nearly every contingency, with one startling exception: no provision was made for a Secretary of Fine Arts or Education. This was an omission of consequence. Every other civilized country had a Minister of Arts, and the countries that were relatively uncivilized had high priests who took care of these matters. Even the most ancient and primitive countries believed art, music, and the theater so important, so involved with their religion and well-being, that they always provided for someone close to the ruler to watch over these affairs. We alone did not.

When Elssler toured the United States in 1842 a pirated print of Taglioni purported to be Fanny.

Collection of Lillian Moore

Ballet in America

Other men have used art as magic, have worshiped it, cherished it, feared it, or forbidden it. We alone condescended to it. We neglected it. This is a remarkable historic fact.

All art needs protection and patronage, particularly the theater, which requires long periods of training and big investments in scenery and costumes. This was simple to arrange when the actors were kings or high priests. It was different now when no single production or performance could be expected to pay back full costs. In America there were no sponsoring organizations, no gentlemen rich enough to maintain private theaters. Congress was born with its eyes closed to the responsibility; it has yet to open them.

But people will be entertained, and in the 19th century theater, even in this wilderness, began to develop. Traveling players took to the boards with Shakespeare and the standard European classics, giving performances wherever there was a platform and a row of benches. Families of native actors, like the Booths, became famous. There were shortly good theaters in all the eastern cities, some with fine repertory companies. European stars braved the seas and the uncouth local manners. America was growing rich and could pay for treats.

Philadelphia soon became the leading theatrical city, surpassing even New York, with several theaters and regular seasons that included every kind of show: Shakespeare, musical extravaganzas, animal acts, pantomimes, acrobatic displays, and attempts at ballet and opera, frequently all on the same bill.

Since the beginning of the republic there had been sporadic attempts at producing grand opera. Philadelphia and New York began to try the form with increasing frequency. But the greatest of the European divas, Maria Malibran and Giula Grisi, had to bring or form their own companies. Jenny Lind, the most famous of all, appeared only in concert. The opera production and casts available did not tempt her.

There were, outside of New Orleans, no lasting opera or ballet companies, no official lyric theaters or endowed schools. Every manager and teacher worked on his own. But they kept working. And they kept sending invitations abroad.

Teachers came, settling for the most part in Philadelphia. They were at first French people trained at the Opéra. The French Revolution and Napoleonic upsets had finished a number of careers, for the ballet and aristocracy were always closely linked. Under the care of the *émigrés*, pupils of real merit developed: Mary Ann Lee, Julia Turnbull, the superb Augusta Maywood, and our first real male ballet star, George Washington Smith (1820-1899). They performed in ballets remembered by the teacher Hazard from his days at the Opéra. Reproduction of foreign works became the fashion, and bits and pieces of different ballets were inserted or taken out or interchanged at will. Young Smith seems to have been an expert at this carpentry and while he never developed any great originality, his skill at manipulating and adapting were to serve visiting Europeans to good effect.

Smith became with time sufficiently versatile to partner every great female star who came to America for the next fifty years, including several leading Spanish dancers, Pepita Soto among

Program for Elssler's appearance in Boston. All boxes were auctioned off on the night of her seventh appearance.

George Washington Smith (note support behind back and in sleeve)

The exterior and interior of the Park Theatre, New York

others. He excelled in many styles and was an able actor and pantomimist in the classic English tradition, having studied the harlequin attitudes from the great English clown, James Byrne of Drury Lane. Smith was a good actor and joined Edwin Booth's company, dancing hornpipes in between the acts of *Hamlet*. An idea of his technical ability can be grasped from the fact that he often and easily performed entrechat dix and was a master of triple turns in the air.

While Smith was still a youth and struggling to learn, he saw Jules Perrot, who was wandering about in search of the recognition that seemed to elude him. Perrot went to New York and Boston, but there were no companies waiting, and it is not known if he found even an adequate partner. His audience was absolutely unprepared to understand what they were looking at; most of them had seen nothing beyond an Irish reel or Negro minstrel clog. But they could recognize a jump when they saw one, and he was the greatest jumper in the world. The local dancers, including Smith, must have sat with their eyes bugging from their cheeks.

In 1839 at the Park Theatre in New York, Marie Taglioni's brother Paul and his German wife Amalia danced most of the works that their papa had created for sister Marie. Everyone hastened to copy.

In the same year Jean Petipa and his son Marius, the future great choreographer, followed. Like Perrot, they left without accomplishing much in the way of lasting influence. But no matter how disgruntled or personally disappointed these men might have felt, they had done something! Fanny Elssler was about to appear. They had paved the way for her, an achievement, no doubt, quite outside their original intent.

In 1840 the United States was ready for a star. There were enough students to watch with understanding and enough dancers to fill out a company. The public had been told what to expect. The United States had heard much of Marie Taglioni, and had had a taste of her style through her brother and his wife. Taglioni was a world legend, and had become one of the sights of Paris. When visitors made the Grand Tour of palaces and churches they hastened also to see Rachel at the Comédie Française and Taglioni at the Opéra. The letters home were dazzled and enchanted. When Elssler was hailed as Taglioni's rival, it made front page news in New York.

And Elssler kept getting talked about for all sorts of reasons. She was beautiful. She had admirers. That was expected of a ballerina. But Elssler had unusual adventures. On the trip across, a sailor had entered her cabin to steal her jewels. She was alone and unarmed so she did what any ballet dancer would instinctively do: she kicked. Let no one underestimate the strength developed by grand battements and pliés. She killed the man. She was sorry about this, but he had been in the wrong.

Evidently her battements were unimpaired, for when she danced in New York the audience gave her an ovation. So great was the excitement and so arduous the performance that, at the end of the second solo, Fanny fainted dead away in her sister Theresa's arms.

Museum of the City of New York

121

Collection of Lillian Moore

Contemporary music cover

Mary Ann Lee as Beatrix in La Jolie Fille de Gand

Photo Courtesy of Lillian Moore

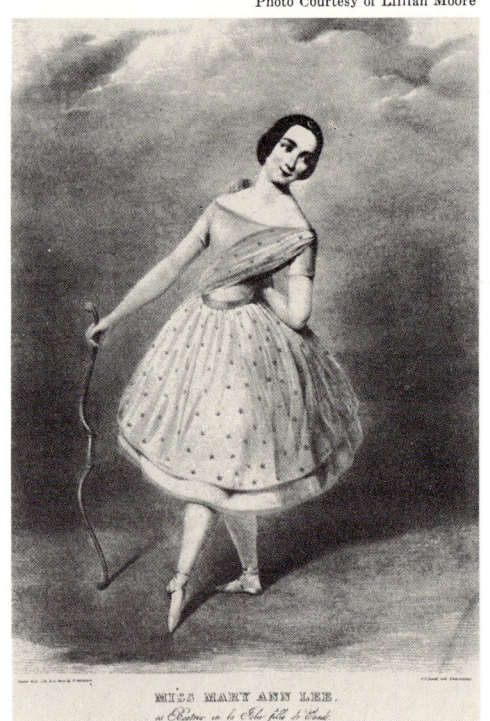

And indeed conditions were difficult. Elssler brought eight full ballets and a number of her most famous variations (short dances). She brought an Irishman, James Sylvian (né Sullivan) as partner and regisseur, and several soloists. She added the best American performers she could find, Julia Turnbull and George Washington Smith among others, recruiting local talent to fill out the corps and turning them over to her Irishman to be whipped into shape, sometimes in only a matter of hours.

The costumes were usually rented and had little to do with each other. But so starved for beauty were the audiences and so devoid of grounds for comparison, that they would rise in a mass and stamp and call out their grateful amazement. They took the horses from her carriage and pulled her through the streets to her hotel, a performance that was duplicated by the United States senators when she danced in Washington. In fact, her triumph there caused Congress to recess for want of a quorum on the nights she performed.

The artists and intellectuals in this country, even such austere and non-theatric people as Margaret Fuller and Ralph Waldo Emerson, were deeply impressed. "This is religion," breathed Miss Fuller in awe. Who could have thought a Spanish dancer in a rose satin skirt could have provoked such a remark from a New England philosopher?

Elssler went home very happy, and very, very rich. She was guaranteed $500.00 per performance, a vast sum in those days, and she toured quite steadily for two years. She left behind enduring and fruitful impressions.

As with any colonial nation (and, though independent politically, we believed ourselves still children in the arts), the entire energy went to copying the older countries' achievements. There was no true creativity in our theater. Mary Ann Lee, who had been to Paris to study, reproduced *Giselle* and several more of the great ballets. She worked entirely from memory, so they may not have been exact, but she did bring back the scores and the scenarios, the style and many of the steps. Both Mary Ann Lee and George Washington Smith had memorized all of Elssler's dances and ballets.

After Elssler, the European parade was on. Any dancer who had a year to spare and was not doing too well at home hurried over. Ballet reached its peak here in the late 1850's. But although many notables visited us, including the troupe of Dominico Ronzani (later the leading choreographer at La Scala), all their efforts came to nothing in the way of provoking a permanent opera or ballet in the New World.

Ballet as it was practiced in Europe was not our natural means of expression any more than grand opera was. We had not the houses or institutions for it, not the state schools or the government patronage, and therefore we had not the means of cultivating public taste.

Our own kind of dancing was developing elsewhere, in the barrooms, tents, and low-grade theaters. But for one hundred years these innovations made no impression at all on the ballet-minded public.

D URING the second half of the 19th century, expression and content were largely suppressed in favor of physical virtuosity.

In spite of the fact that the greatest choreographers and craftsmen of the ballet were men, and that they gave us the only lasting choreographic works the West has known, ballet dancing had become a woman's medium. This was the first theater form in either the East or West to be taken over and exploited by women. Ballets and roles were composed chiefly to reveal their special charms; all men in the field were reduced to subordinate functions —even the great ballet masters. They composed to serve the ballerinas, and the ladies were quite emphatically not preoccupied with either spiritual or emotional values.

Jumping lifts were developed, multiple finger turns, and longer, stronger point work. The ballet slipper began to be stiffened slightly to support grinding demands. It was not yet, however, the hard shoe we use today. Pantomime remained formal and separate from the dance proper.

Fokine writes of the methods which prevailed before he took over: "The pantomime scenes were staged in accordance with a specific gesture language. When it became necessary to express with gestures the phrase 'Call the Judge here,' Ivanov began to think out loud: 'How do you say "Judge?" "Call" is simple. "Here" is simpler still. But how does one say "Judge" in gestures?' He fretted, toyed with his long upraised palms of his hands up and down in front of his face. 'I have it! These are the scales, the scales of Justice—"Judge!"'"

(This, of course, is straight charades. We play it today in a parlor exercise called The Game.)

In its most effective form this kind of acting crystallized in the pantomime scene of ballets like *Swan Lake, Don Quixote,* and *The Sleeping Beauty.*

In 1887 the Italian ballerina Pierina Legnani (1863-1923), who had trained in Milan, brought her superb technical inventions to the Czar's theater in St. Petersburg. She was one of the two dancers in Russian history to be accorded the title "Prima Ballerina Assoluta." Legnani first turned thirty-two fouetté pirouettes in *The Tulip of Haarlem* (1893). Fouetté pirouettes are a stunt consisting of repeated turns on one leg, the heel resting on the floor between each revolution and the body whipped around by the pumping motion of the free leg. The rapidity and duration of execution constitute the brilliance of the feat. Legnani could do thirty-two in the space of a ruble marked out for her toe on the floor. The Russian ballet master Legat records that by watching her carefully he was able to teach the trick to Mathilde Kschessinskaya, who became the first Russian dancer to execute the complete set. Since then, no girl has had any peace. It is the great double dare; it is the four-minute mile, the goal being sixty-four done in one spot—on the whole, rather too many.

Now every seven-year student—particularly Americans, who are adroit at turns—insists on attempting them, thirty-two if not sixty-four.

The Decline

The men dancers were used mainly for lifting. They were called "porteurs." It wasn't considered much of a profession. Self-respecting men wouldn't go into it. In France and England the men's roles began to be played by women, which made the whole business very silly.

The men dancers didn't think much of the women and the women didn't think much of the men. Manners deteriorated. Also work.

Acting was not only stylized to an almost Oriental degree, all expression and appearance was stilted and designed for show. The ballerinas sought to dazzle by the crudest means and preferred diamonds to emotion. Retired, in her old age, Taglioni deplored this. "She notices, in looking at ballets, how often the dancers put on a smile and wear it, just as they put ornaments in their hair; and she herself supposes some part of her marvellous power over the public to have lain in the fact that her smiles were never put on, but sprang spontaneously out of the joy which the delight of movement created in her," wrote Mable Cross in the *University Magazine* in 1879.

Above: the beginning of a bad trend, Miss Fairbrother as Aladdin, c.1830.

Below: Lea Piron as Franz, the leading male role in Coppélia, *Paris Opéra.*

A stage of roses and beauty. All male roles taken by women.

A typical pas de deux at the turn of the century.

be permitted to stop laughing and to express sadness, or wistfulness, or despair. Up to that point the Negro entertainer was only tolerated in public if he was jolly or comic. But Juba, and all the people who followed him, together with their music, were recognized universally as exponents of our most characteristic theater expression.

There have been great followers who developed an enormous body of technique, a remarkable handling of rhythm and posture, and a kind of surprising humor, an impertinence, and above all a physical exuberance, a hell-for-leather joy, that was deep-down, through and through American. "Jim Crow" Rice, whose limp in Rocking De Heel started a vogue; two black-face artists of the seventies, Dan Bryant, who tapped slowly, and George F. More, who invented soft shoe; the unknowns who gave us the Essence, the Sand Dance, Buck and Wing, the Cakewalk, the Pedestal Dance; Harry Bolger, who invented slap shoe; Eddie Foy, the Hand Dance; Eddie Horan, the Cane Dance; Bill "Bojangles" Robinson, Peg Leg Bates, Fred Astaire, Ray Bolger, Gene Kelly, Paul Draper. The great stars in this field, as opposed to ballet, have all been men. Tapping and jazz are essentially a male form of dancing. The stigma attached to male dancing in the United States has never at any time related to this form. It is beyond suspicion.

The dancers who took over the popular theater during the first part of our century were soloists, and the arrangements and choreography were for the solo figure, but about fifty years ago choruses of clogging, tapping, step, and soft-shoe dancing began to be popular. The thirty-two Rockettes, who do precision high kicks and fairly complex tap, became as peculiarly a New York attraction as the noise and high buildings. These were not, however, real developments of the tap technique. All effects were achieved by the simple multiplication of the solo dancer, identical and in brigade formations. Complex group patterns in this promising and lively technique remain to be attempted.

There is a wide breach, however, between indigenous American theater forms, such as jazz and tap dancing, and our other theater styles. In Europe, a similar divergence does not hold true. Classic ballet developed from the European folk forms and is therefore basically related to them. It can incorporate native steps without any great loss of style, even including versions of Spanish dances. But tap dancing and ballet have no roots in common. This fact has tended to keep them from merging in any way.

Also, each has an extremely difficult technique. The ballet dancer needs a tight foot and controlled ankle, the tap dancer a relaxed foot and loose ankle. The ballet dancer uses a straight stiffened knee, the tap dancer a loose knee.

Today there are only a few people outstanding in both styles: Frederic Franklin (strangely enough, an Englishman), Tommy Rall, Harold Lang, Danny Daniels.

During waxings and wanings of ballet popularity, through all the phases of two hundred years of theater, the popular entertainments persisted, the clowns, the acrobats, and the café and vaudeville dancers. These follow an old tradition. They invent new surprises when they can. But they tend to be cautious. Whatever

Elliott & Fry

Adeline Genée as La Carmargo "...triumphant and provocative... like an incredible living jewel in the deep gloom of the stage."
ARNOLD BENNETT

Bill "Bojangles" Robinson

Twentieth Century-Fox

*Jane Avril
by Toulouse Lautrec*

Photo Wildenstein, New York

Mabel Love

Culver Pictures, Inc.

*English
music hall girls*

Le Théatre

they think of must be tested right away on an audience that stands no nonsense. There are no endowments for them. Few great works, therefore, come out of this theater, few works that last beyond the lifetime of the performers, but there is always vitality and clarity and presence. And there is never any great bother about making or breaking rules. Here there is one rule: Don't be a bore.

The tradition of the clowns and jokesters begins with the ancient totem animal dances, continues through the Greek and Roman theaters (satyrs, spirits, servants, common or weak mortals) down through the devils of the medieval mysteries to the great pantomime clowns and improvisations of the Commedia dell'Arte. These people were not dancers proper, but they worked with music and stylized gesture. They worked alongside dancers. They were the link between the high theater, opera and tragedy, and the common people—a sort of leavening. Today they survive in circuses, popular musical theaters, movies, and TV.

They usually wear a grotesque and individual make-up, the mark of their own personality, and they seldom vary it. Costume and painted face become a mask through which they function. This unchanging disguise constitutes, in the words of Walter Kerr, "...what all honest theater men have been trying to achieve since the wholly rigid mask was formally dropped. They offer us a vision of both the man and the mask in the same, or nearly the same, instant. The private, personal soul is made visible; but over it and across it like light reflected in a window-pane shimmers the universal grimace, the grimace of common terror or common joy that links so many unique and lonely figures in a vast and universal chain. The one and the many are on top in a single, blinding rush of energy, implying one another, reinforcing one another...."

The great clowns of the last hundred and fifty years, mostly men, have been deeply loved by multitudes all over the world. Many of them have become millionaires. They have in time influenced the dancers and musicians in the great opera houses. Many a "stunt," successful in the "halls," has become an "effect" in the opera.

*Colette Willy,
later the famous author,
in her vaudeville version
of an Egyptian dance*

Among the most-loved popular dancers of the last century were Letty Lind and Kate Vaughn of the English variety halls, who were superb skirt dancers. Skirt dancing consisted of graceful semi-balletic steps, without the big jumps and without point work or lifts. The dancers waved and rustled extremely full skirts. Kate Vaughn also did high kicks and beautiful work with a tambourine. She coached Jane Avril, the Paris can-can dancer.

The American Loie Fuller made a spectacular act out of skirt dancing by wearing skirts one hundred yards round and manipulating them with sticks under the play of colored lights. From her example stems a whole school of scarf-waving, cloth-swishing, veil-tossing performances that have trapped many people who should know better.

Burning of the Park Theatre in New York, 1848

The tragic burning of Emma Livry, favorite pupil of Taglioni, who died as a result of her costume catching fire during a rehearsal, Opéra, 1862.

Fuller was the first person to experiment with moving lights. She was able to do this because electric light had been invented, the first safe lighting in the theater. Candle and gas footlights had caused many a death through burning. The average life of an 18th- or 19th-century opera house was thirty years. With electricity, lights could safely be turned on and off, moved and varied in intensity. This change has affected dance style and, to an enormous degree, scenery and costumes, which now tend to be less elaborate, more mobile, simple, and suggestive.

This then was the state of dancing at the turn of the century, lively enough fun in the flourishing commercial halls, decadent, repetitious, and withered in the opera houses, until one woman came along to change history.

Fire *by Loie Fuller*

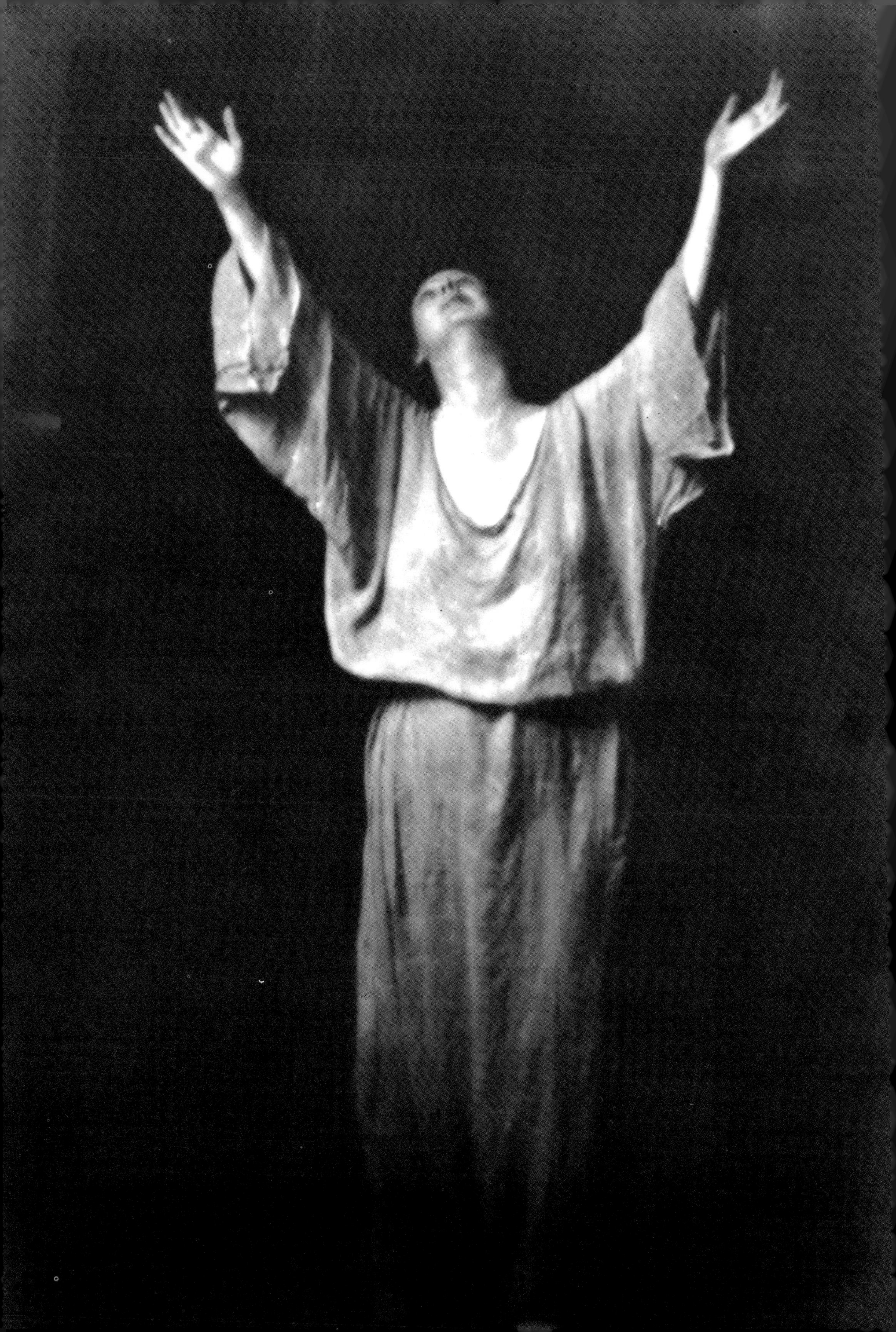

AT the turn of the century Isadora Duncan (1878-1927), a San Francisco girl who believed that dancing was heading up a blind alley, threw off her corsets and her shoes and danced barefoot across Europe. Her effect on contemporaries and successors has been incalculable.

Isadora left not one single enduring work in the repertory of any company, nor any addition to the code of technique. Some even think her style "little more than a misdirection." What we inherit is a point of view, a sense of dignity and passion, where before there was none, a tradition of glory in a field long soiled and shabby.

Before Isadora, dancing was not considered important or dignified, except by the people who practiced it; after her, it came to be. This was her contribution.

She placed dancing on a par with religion, reversing two thousand years of frivolity. She returned to the ancient concept of dance as the mother of the arts, dance as a form of worship.

She believed dancing should be harmonious and simple, that is, stripped of all needless ornamentation. She herself performed without scenery, using only curtains and lights. Her costumes were simple tunics and scarves.

There was nothing simple about her music. She danced only to the greatest. Musicians were at first shocked, but she continued and convinced them. Great music, she said, dictated great dancing. She turned to classic Greek mythology for her subjects, not in the spirit of masquerades with the vanity of the French kings, but believingly and humbly as the ancients did. She scorned the late 19th-century attitude that a dancing career was only for unfortunate girls and lower class boys, or merely a contest in acrobatic tricks.

She did not, as is popularly supposed, discover a new type of dance, nor yet revive an ancient one. Her style has been called Greek simply because she chose to wear Greek tunics and referred always, when speaking, to classic sources. But her idiom was no more Greek than anything else. It was her own personal way of expression and for this reason it has not proved lasting, except as an influence. She invented no steps.

She did not evolve her great style entirely without precedent. François Delsarte (1811-1871) had analyzed the gestures and postures of the body for expression as musicians had analyzed voice and speech. Jacques Dalcroze (1865-1950) had related movement to rhythm scientifically, and a century of pantomime and posturings in imitation of great paintings and statues had preceded her, beginning with Sarah Siddons and Emma, Lady Hamilton, and involving very nearly every aesthetically inclined lady at the great 19th-century house-parties. Duncan went on from there.

Her achievement was a point of view. She cleared away the accumulated debris of six hundred years of artificiality. Ballet dancing had become corrupt. She left it, though unintentionally (she had hoped to destroy it utterly), honest and meaningful.

Isadora Duncan by Bakst

Duncan

Two of Isadora's adopted daughters and disciples, Theresa, above, and Anna.

She rediscovered the human walk, the run, the easy natural spring and jump, the emotional use of head and arms and hands. Her basic theory was that all movement derives from simple walking, running, skipping, jumping, and standing. She believed that these movements could be exciting and satisfying in themselves, without distortion, without the turning out of legs and pointing of toes and the holding of arms in symmetrical rounded ballet positions. She said all movement should be examined for purity and strength, that to be merely traditional meant nothing. She reminded us we come of a democratic country with a free point of view, and should bow to nothing but our own ideal of beauty.

She brought the foot once more into contact with the earth. She bared the limbs so that we might see not so much the naked body as revealed emotion. She rediscovered spontaneity and individual passion. She was to her art what Luther was to the Medieval Church: she questioned.

But in throwing away both distortions and formal technique, she dismissed what no art can long endure without. Distortion is a kind of preservative; like the mask, it covers naked sentiment, bare personality, and makes emotion communicable and lasting. It is only when it is practiced for its own sake that it cancels emotion.

But it is good for us to examine the style of any art from time to time and clean out what has grown lifeless. Isadora was like a broom. She worked the briskest theater-sweeping the world has ever seen.

She cleared away square miles of painted scenery. Under her championship simple architectural forms, curtains, and lights became important. She swept away all fancy and ornate costumes. Simplicity, which means a choice of what is absolutely essential, returned. Where spectacle had been all powerful, imagination, evocation, and symbolism, as the Orientals and ancients used them, returned. Not since the Elizabethans had there been such an honest, bare stage.

She not only cleaned away rubbish; she opened the windows and ventilated what had been foul and evil-smelling.

She believed that dancing was proper for everyone, regardless of class or social standing. Now women of probity and intellect began to join the profession.

But there were drawbacks to her plan. Her style, unfortunately, was easier to fake than others. She herself was a perfectionist, but people misunderstood her. What was chiefly wanted, women gathered, was a spiritual preparation but no special technique to speak of—off with the shoes, down with self-criticism, and away to the strains of Schubert. They called this self-indulgence "Interpretive Dancing." It swept three continents and two generations, all female. Men are never quite so silly, or not in just this way.

But art is not easy. It is the audience who must do the feeling, and they always need convincing. Interpretive dancing was, however, good for women's nerves, as tennis or golf is good for men's.

Isadora preached a gospel of freedom and happiness for women in all aspects of life. She wanted them to be released from the restrictions, legal and domestic, that had held them down for thousands of years.

She appeared at a time when there was beginning to be felt a world-wide interest in bettering women's position, in giving them the vote, in permitting them to hold public office, in opening to them careers in medicine and law, in guaranteeing them legal rights to and control over their children, in permitting them to own their own money. Isadora talked to a rising tide of interest and conviction.

She reformed women's dress in everyday life, and so indirectly their way of living. She cried out against corsets, petticoats, button-boots, feather hats, false hair, heavy skirts, high-heeled shoes. Many women were in similar open protest, including several famous and fashionable dancers like Irene Castle, but Isadora cried the loudest and the most publicly. The clothes she advocated made possible modern sports for women and this meant a great improvement in women's health and child-bearing capacity. The sweater girl, free-walking, free-running, naked in bathing and brown in the sun, is Isadora's bequest.

She preached the basics: Dress sensibly. Move freely. Keep healthy. Consider yourself no one's slave—not even your husband's. Express your emotions deeply and freely in art.

No wonder women were excited by what she said. No wonder they wept and cheered and threw flowers whenever she danced.

She died in an auto accident a relatively young woman, 48, but she left disciples and pupils all over Europe and America. She adopted daughters who carried on her work, Anna, Lise, Margot, Erica, Theresa, Irma, but all the dancers who came after are, in a sense, her children.

She touched off a creative conflagration. Not since the discovery of ancient statues during the Renaissance had such a re-evaluation of standards been witnessed in the arts. She preached a return to classic simplicity and pagan joy at the precise moment in history when our civilization was moving forward into a new era, when freedoms of all kinds were being sought—economic, political, social, and spiritual.

Duncan by Grandjouan
Dance Collection of Arthur Todd

Three of the "Isadorables," Margo, Anna, and Irma.
N. Y. Public Library Dance Collection, Irma Duncan Collection

Fokine by V. Sérow

Bibliothèque du Conservatoire, Paris

Fokine

THE American theater could not profit by Isadora Duncan's great example because in the matter of dancing the American theater was completely disorganized. There were no fine companies of trained professionals to keep standards high; amateurs copied only her eccentricities; professionals copied the worn-out tricks of Europe. It was in Europe, ironically enough, that she had her strongest professional influence.

The Russian, Michael Fokine (1880-1942), was the first great choreographer to respond directly to Duncan's influence.

When he saw Duncan he knew that what he had dreamt of doing was possible. And although he was a classicist, bred and schooled at the Imperial Russian Ballet in St. Petersburg, he began choreographing in a way that was altogether different from that of the masters who had preceded him. It was Fokine who realized in full the innovations Noverre had begged for one hundred and sixty years before and for which Perrot had struggled so hard. But the direct inspiration, the spark that fired Fokine's genius, was the barefoot, tunic-clad, Isadora on a bald stage, dancing alone to Beethoven.

He had long been ready for change, and new ideas and schemes were fermenting in his mind. The state of things in the ballet world sickened him.

"...The pas de deux we executed in these ballets remain much more vividly in my memory. The choreography for those we mostly staged ourselves. In a sense they cannot be labeled as compositions at all. We did whatever we felt we could do best. I did high jumps and Pavlova pirouettes. There was no connection whatsoever between our 'number' and the ballet into which it was inserted. Neither was there any connection with the music. We began our adagio when the music began and finished when the music came to an end. The interval between the beginning and the end was spent in carefree floating, totally disregarding the musical phrasing. During such a pas de deux Pavlova would say to me, 'Take it easy, we still have a great deal of music left,' or 'Hurry, hurry!'—whichever the case might be. Towards the end of such an adagio we would invariably walk downstage, always in the center, she on her toes with her eyes fixed on the conductor and I following behind with my eyes focused on her waist, prepared for the expected catch. [This was to end the final pirouette.]

" 'Don't forget the push,' she would whisper softly.

"After the performance I would pose this question to myself: Is this all necessary? What does it mean?...And it would become very clear to me that all this was unnecessary and meant nothing.

"I realized that the audience could not possibly believe that in any sincerity of interpretation and projection from the artists when such artists, portraying a couple in love, acted as though completely oblivious of each other, focusing their pleading gaze at the balcony....

"We, the male classic dancers, also did not have either the appearance or the manners required by our roles.... In fact, each dance was nothing more than a demonstration of agility and virtuosity. The very designation 'classic' dancer as opposed to 'character' dancer betrayed the fact that the conveying of character—no matter of what type—was not included in our requirements."

Shortly after Duncan's appearance in St. Petersburg, part of the Russian Ballet left home and came west in 1909 under the direction of Serge Diaghileff (1872-1929). They brought a galaxy of genius and inaugurated an era of creativity without parallel.

The Parisians had got used to women masquerading as men. "The art of the dance has fallen into complete decadence in our country," wrote Marcel Prévost "...une sorte de convention de laisser aller s'est établie entre les artistes et le public. Des prêtresses sans foi accomplissent au petit bonheur des rites périmés devant des fidèles sceptiques et distraits." But now with the advent of the Russians, for the first time in two generations of dancers, they saw great male performers and the uninhibited wildness and excitement of the Russian folk dances. Paris had not within memory witnessed such a synthesis of drama, music, color, and choreography. The dance renaissance had begun.

Fokine and Diaghileff followed Duncan's lead in the matter of using great music. By the mid-19th century it had become increasingly the vogue to use light and trivial music, Tchaikowsky's scores being the only exception. Fokine and Diaghileff drew on Schumann, Moussorgsky, Scarlatti, Chopin, Cimarosa, and the fine moderns: Stravinsky, Debussy, Ravel, Borodin, and Rimski-Korsakov. Dancers now were called on to understand the phrasing of complicated rhythmic patterns. There was to be no more counting everything out regularly in groups of eight; dancers now must bruise their memories on Stravinsky.

Duncan had thrown away painted scenery and elaborate costumes. Diaghileff reintroduced paint but only by the greatest artists, and with color such as the West had never seen in their theater. The leading designer, Leon Bakst, borrowing from the Orient, opened the eyes of Europe. The browns, the buffs, and the dull greens and the drab roses of the 19th century suddenly looked like old clothes. First the Diaghileff Ballet, then the theater of the world, flamed with color. A very clear idea of what the 19th-century theater looked like before Fokine and Bakst can be seen in the contemporary Bolshoi productions.

Under Fokine both scenery and costumes were designed by one man, an innovation at the time.

Like Noverre, he insisted that the style or idiom of each ballet be suited to the subject and varied with each subject. He refused to make do with combinations of ready-made and established dance steps.

He insisted that no dance be inserted unless it served the overall dramatic purpose.

He broke the Petipa formula of three or more acts and produced one-act ballets of concentrated dramatic action and power.

He discarded the rigid pattern of parade entry, pantomime, solo variations, chorus dance, star turn, and final parade, and used

First poster of Diaghileff's Ballet Russes in Paris: Anna Pavlova in Fokine's Les Sylphides.

Stravinsky with Nijinsky costumed for Petrouchka

Musée des Arts Décoratifs, Paris. Photo du Musée

Decor and a costume for Schéhérazade *by Bakst*

instead any order and sequence that told the story best. The traditional third act, with its marches and short dances or variations, was doomed. He worked without formula. The leading characters carried the dramatic action and the chorus expanded and reflected their emotion, exactly as in a play.

He demanded acting and real characterization from his performers. Mime became clear, less like sign language. "Man should be expressive from head to foot," he said. It was no longer necessary for the audience to serve an apprenticeship to understand what the dancers were saying.

Bottom two illustrations:
Wadsworth Atheneum, Hartford, The Ella Gallup Sumner and Mary Catlin Sumner Collection

Karsavina's costume for Le Spectre de la Rose *by Benois*

140

*Officer's costume
for* Petrouchka
by Benois

Decor for La Pavillon d'Armide *by Benois*

Decor for Les Sylphides
by Braque

From V. Svetlov. "Le Ballet Contemporain."
de Brunhoff, Editeur. Paris 1912

Top three illustrations:
Wadsworth Atheneum, Hartford, The Ella Gallup Sumner
and Mary Catlin Sumner Collection

*Costume for the Doll
and the decor for* Petrouchka
by Benois

From V. Svetlov. "Le Ballet Contemporain."
de Brunhoff, Editeur. Paris 1912

Bacchanales *before and after Duncan.*
Top: *Marie M. Petipa and P. A. Gerdt,*
choreography by her father,
Marius Petipa;
below: *Pavlova and Mikhail Mordkin,*
choreography by Fokine.

Photo Courtesy of Lillian Moore

"It is difficult to express in words the difference between the way I staged 'Scheherazade' in my own new style and the manner in which it would have been presented according to the old classic formula. I will, however, try to describe it.

"How would the pantomime scene have been staged before? This is the scene: Shah Zeman sees his brother Shah Shahryar order the slaughter of all his wives, but hesitate over the order to kill his favorite wife, Zobeide, because he loves her and is sorry for her. Shah Zeman is indignant at his brother's weakness and is ashamed of him.

"What would he do at this point according to the traditional pantomime formula of the classic ballet? First of all, he would walk around the stage in a circle (this was a must, in order to draw the attention of the audience)....

"There would follow this pantomimic monologue: 'When...' (the artist would say this to himself but not express it in any way) 'the night descends...' (making a severe face the artist would lean slightly forward, placing his arms over his head to signify 'cover of darkness') 'here...' (pointing his index finger to the floor) 'come...' (he would walk a few paces, pointing his finger in various directions at the end of each walking step) 'one, two, three...' (first shows one finger, then two fingers, then three) 'Negroes' (assuming an angry look to convey the dark color, while the hand goes over his face in a downward gesture suggesting sunset, emphasizing darkness) and so on. According to this system, which is too long to describe completely here, the pantomime language expressed not what was necessary but what was possible. So, if the Shah had played by traditional rules, he would have gone through hundreds of unnecessary gestures with his hands.

"Instead, my Shah Zeman gravely approached the corpse of the Favorite Slave, Zobeide's lover. He rolled him over and then put his foot on the body and, with his hand, indicated the dead man to Shah Shahryar. That was all."

Fokine had the dancers turn their backs. "It is now difficult to realize to what a degree dancers once feared to show their backs to the audience. This had its origin in the court ballets, where walking backwards was done in order to remain in the position of constantly facing some exalted personage in the audience.

"...Having ceased to dance for the audience, the new ballet began to dance for itself and the surrounding people. The new approach not only enriched the dance, but freed it from the ugliness inescapably connected with the necessity of walking backwards and sidestepping."

Fokine expanded the classic technique to include freer arm movements, freer and swifter leg movements, and a more supple back. Ballet dancing was now often wild and rhapsodic and always free-flowing. The arms seemed to lift from the base of the spine, the legs moved with total body force, with the stretching of the full skeleton. Emphasis was removed from feet and finger-tips; movement embraced everything. "No one in my ballets has a stiff neck," he said to Nina Stragonova, giving her a push. "Move!"

He broke the rigid rules for arm and head positions. He felt that what was meaningful was correct for any given ballet. Because he was steeped in traditional ballet training, the body lines remained basically classic, but dancers were no longer dainty. They were fleet, strong, and impassioned. Today, Galina Ulanova is probably the greatest living exponent of his style, although she did not study under him.

None of the mid-century ballerinas could have moved with this freedom or fluidity. Nor would they have wanted to. They would have considered it unwomanly, almost brutal. Their gestures had remained, no matter what the strength expended, symmetrical, self-embracing and decorous. It used to be the very decorum of the step that excited men, the masking of the great strength. Fokine wished to excite them with abandon.

He introduced asymmetry, permitting the hips to relax in uneven line, the spine to curve. He relaxed the knee as in ancient sculptures and taught dancers to walk simply—straight forward and not splay-footed in a duck-waddle, like the old-fashioned ballet dancers.

He borrowed from folk forms, not just by inserting strings of pretty little folk dances from different countries, but by adapting and expanding the basic native style.

He discarded the classic tutu (Taglioni's ballet skirt) and the traditional male tights. Dancers now wore anything suitable.

He brought back the male dancer as a central figure. Never before in the Western theater, not even in the days of Vestris, had men dancers held such a dominant role. No wonder the fashionable world of Paris rocked at his revelations.

Tamara Karsavina writes in *Theater Street*: "A vivid, if somewhat unrefined, account of what was happening in the audience when Nijinsky and I danced...on the first night I will borrow from Michael, our courier...'But when these two came on, good Lord! I have never seen such a public. You would have thought their seats were on fire.'"

"After the Polovetzian Dances," wrote Fokine, "the audience rushed forward and actually tore off the orchestra rail in the Chatelet Theater....The success was absolutely unbelievable." Diaghileff characterized the moment: "We're all living in the witchery of Armida's groves. The very air round the Russian season is intoxicated."

Karsavina continues: "A truer definition of the atmosphere enveloping the Russian season and its audience could not have been found, a subtle, light, gay intoxication. Something akin to a miracle happened every night—the stage and audience trembled in a unison of emotion....

"In Diaghileff's small flat beat the pulse of his formidable enterprise. Strategic moves and counter-moves of his ingenuity, planning, budgeting, music in one corner, discussion in another. A Chancery and a small Parnassus in the restricted space of two rooms. The lines of each production were discussed there first. Around the table sat wise men; the Artistic Committee drinking weak tea and hatching daring ideas. Quite unrepeatable were those days, unimaginable the boyish exuberance of these pioneers of Russian art. However much experience was gained in latter years, nothing can bring back that early enthusiasm...."

*Karsavina and Bolm
in Fokine's* Thamar

*Karsavina and Nijinsky
in Fokine's* Spectre de la Rose

The decor for Diaghileff's Firebird *was by A. Golovine and the costumes were by Bakst. Karsavina and Fokine created the original roles and Margot Fonteyn danced in the Sadler's Wells revival in 1954.*

"From the top to the bottom, from the priests of art down to each humble servant spread the spirit of reverential eagerness. Even our wig maker and his assistant felt themselves in their jobs, not mere artisans....

"Diaghileff...brought quick, unhesitating decision to every doubt. He had the sense of the theater to an uncanny degree. Engrossed as he was in his part he kept a vigilant eye on his collaborators: 'Gentlemen, you are wandering off your point,' came now and then from his corner. Mortal limitations alone frustrated his brave attempt at omnipresence. For it was Diaghileff's will that set in motion every cog and wheel of the unwieldy machine of his season."

These early Fokine-Diaghileff seasons have probably never been surpassed for excitement and discovery. Tyrone Guthrie speaks of the effect of the Diaghileff Ballet on England during the war years, 1914-1918:

Rembrandt-Rankfilm Verlag from "Ballet International" by H. Koegler, Berlin

"Indeed what everybody wanted almost as much as food or drink during these years was to see youthful creatures beautifully moving through ordered evolutions to a predestined and satisfactory close. It was the antidote to the drabness and dullness and monotony of a life which seemed to be moving in disorder to a predestined and highly unsatisfactory close."

Fokine, within the scope of his innovations, transformed ballet from a pretty entertainment, the mere vehicle of attractive personalities, to a major form of theater.

In many senses he worked like an Elizabethan, translating into his medium the great excitements and impulses of the several arts that were just then reaching the full flux of creative expansion.

At the end of the 19th century, ballets had become formula. He left them original dramatic works of wide range and force.

Fokine composed over sixty ballets. Those that can still be seen show, after fifty years, no age or staleness.

The lapse of twenty-two years between *Le Coq d'Or* (1914), his last ballet-opera for Diaghileff, and the next important work for René Blum's Ballet Russe de Monte Carlo, *L'Epreuve d'Amour* (1936), is explained by the fact that he had no company to work with. In 1912, Diaghileff replaced him as choreographer with Nijinsky. Fokine was a White Russian and could not return to his home theater after the Bolshevik Revolution in 1917. He worked as a guest choreographer for periods with the opera-ballets in Copenhagen, Paris, and Buenos Aires, and tried to form and establish his own troupe in New York. None of these companies provided him with an adequate instrument for the creation of great new works. The best he could do was to restage his old masterpieces. This unfortunate situation occurred when his abilities had reached full creative expression, when his technique had matured and his teaching and directing could call on any collaboration he named; it proved a tragic loss to the whole world of dancing. Had he been enabled to continue his extraordinary career undisturbed and unfrustrated, he might have given us ten more great works.

He has been plagiarized more thoroughly than any other choreographer. There are no laws to prevent the theft of dance compositions, and Fokine saw every representative company performing his works without payment of royalties. Anna Pavlova performed an earlier version of the work *Les Sylphides,* altering the solo passages to suit her technique and wishes as single star. (The Diaghileff version calls for four soloists, three women and a man.) No ballet company in the world is without its version of *Sylphides.* In time a dozen companies performed *Firebird, Schéhérazade, Prince Igor, Spectre de la Rose,* and *Carnaval,* not even always with credit, and only occasionally with exact care for the steps. His autobiography is a prolonged cry of agony for the violence done his works. Finally in 1933 Dame Ninette de Valois called several impresarios together and they agreed voluntarily to pay Fokine a small performing fee for all his choreography. In the meantime, his masterpieces had for the past thirty years been presented in the opera houses of Europe and the Americas nearly as often as Verdi. He was not a penny richer for it, and he died an embittered man.

Ballet owes him an irreparable debt.

Top three illustrations:
From V. Svetlov. "Le Ballet Contemporain."
de Brunhoff, Editeur. Paris 1912

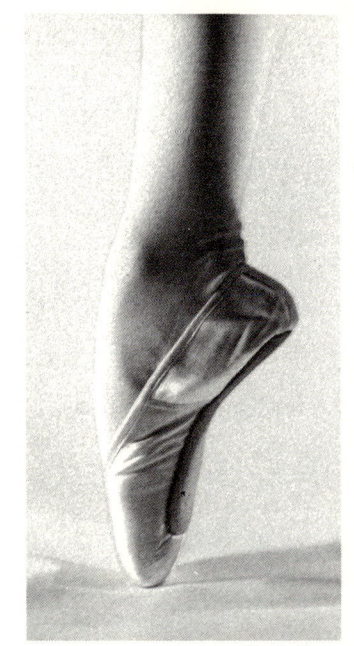

Martha Swope

Markova's foot

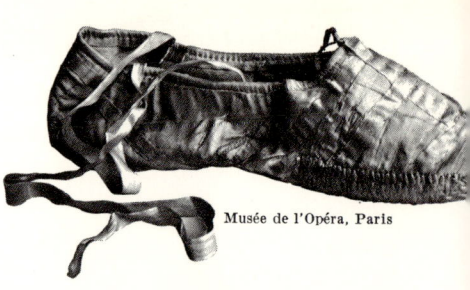

The unblocked slippers
of Taglioni and Emma Livry

Musée de l'Opéra, Paris

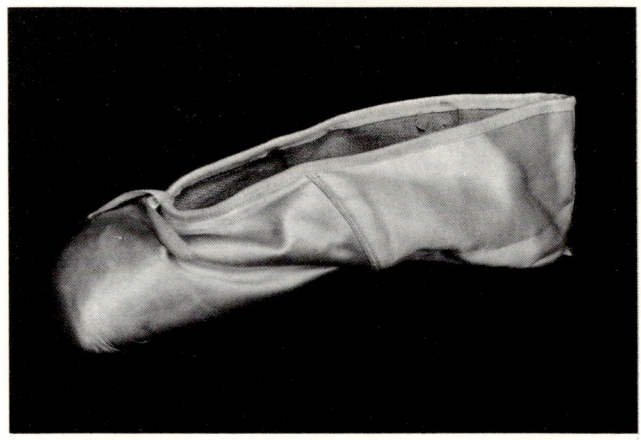

Musée de l'Opéra, Paris

Martha Swope

It takes a dancer about twelve
years to make legs and feet
like these. It took dancing 200
years to learn how. The legs of
Felia Doubrovska.

N. Y. Public Library Dance Collection

A cast of
Pavlova's foot

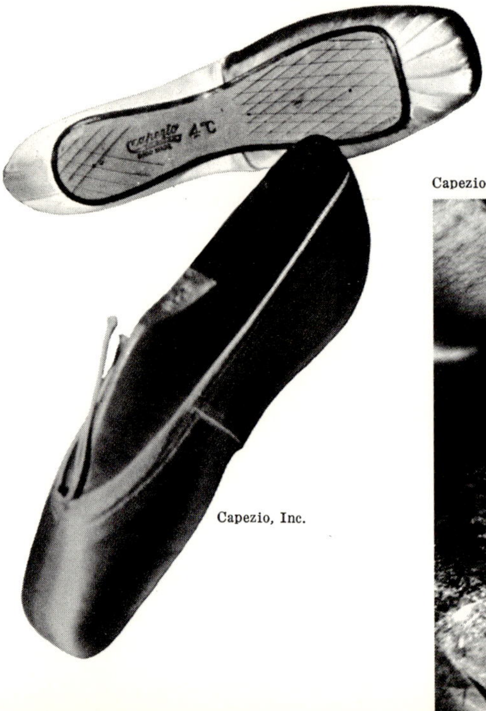

Musee de l'Opéra, Paris

Pavlova's shoe, 1920, stiffer
and blocked, but light and not
nearly so stiff as the
contemporary *assoluta* of Capezio
to the left and being made below.

Capezio, Inc.

Capezio, Inc.

146

Since the advent of Fokine, every ballet dancer has been required to know many styles and to control a remarkable range of gesture. The bodies themselves have changed.

The ballet dancer today is no longer dumpy, but slender and long-limbed—long arms and legs with a short, compact torso. She tends to be underweight and with the figure of a sub-adolescent.

Under Fokine the ballet face became quiet, alert, disciplined, and serene: the modern mask. All emotion has been driven from the countenance into the complete dance gesture. The ballet dancer does not ever grimace. She smiles only when it is appropriate to smile. She does not strive unduly to please; she pleases—or she leaves the theater.

The hand is quiet and more relaxed than formerly. The foot is strong, but possibly not so strong as the 19th-century foot. When no stiffening was used in the slipper for point work, enormous demands were made on instep, ankle, and leg.

The Italian and Danish leg used to be lumpy with muscles and thick in the ankle. This was partly due to point work without artificial aid and partly to the old sequence of practice exercises—the barre used to begin with high battements. The Russians changed this and put the battements at the end. We owe our slender legs to the Russians. A fat calf is not tolerated today.

The modern shoe is not only stronger and tougher than the earlier shoe to support the growing technical demands, it is also larger, longer, and broader, because our skeleton is bigger today than it was 100 years ago—probably due to diet.

Today's shoe makes a knocking sound because of the stiffening of glue and canvas on the ends, and is quite heavy—weighs 4½ ounces (size 4B).

Marie Taglioni's shoe was nearly weightless and soundless. The slipper in which her pupil Emma Livry was burned to death in 1862 weighed one ounce. Anna Pavlova's slipper weighed two ounces.

Some ballerinas prefer their shoes soft enough to enable them to feel the floor through the ends. This can be painful but it makes for feather-lightness and a wonderful flexibility of the arch.

It was not until the beginning of the 20th century that stiffening in the toes was considered anything but vulgar and exhibitionistic. Circus riders and music hall performers stiffened their slippers artificially, but the real artist, the opera dancer, did without mechanical aids, took the brunt on unprotected flesh and with her muscles and craft alone accomplished her technical feats. If her feet bled, they bled; no blocks were permitted. Last century's dancer looked on such mechanical reinforcement very much as a properly trained singer regards a microphone or an instrumentalist an electric guitar or violin.

Taglioni's shoe cost a few sous. She threw them away after every first wearing. The American point or blocked shoe costs $7.95 and the dancer hopes that with care it will last a week.

The making of ballet slippers is a special craft; not as highly skilled or rare as the making of good violins, but important and respected by the people whose success is modified by the shoes

Photo from "Le Ballet" by Boris Kochno and Maria Luz, Art du Monde. Hachette

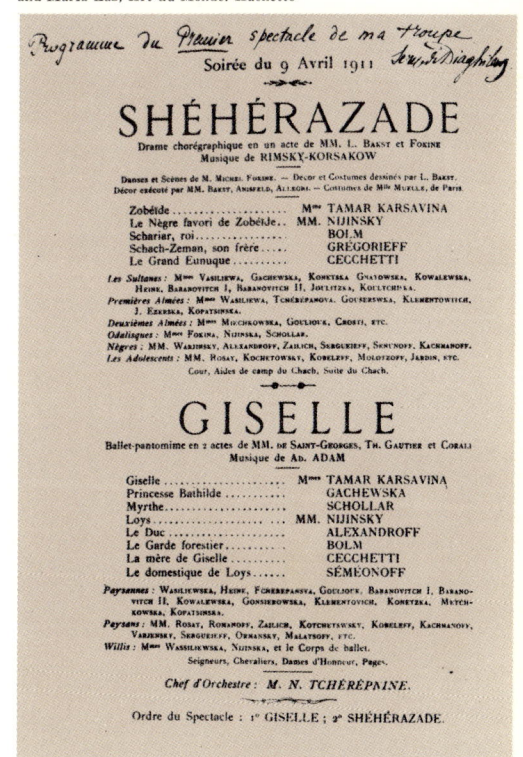

The Stars of the Diaghileff Ballet

they wear. There have been famous slipper-cobblers, mainly Italian. Nicolini supplied Pavlova's point shoes (she bought them by the trunk load and carried them around the world with her). Others include Anello and David, Salvatore Capezio, and Georges (a Russian) who outfitted most contemporary stars. Stars have custom-made slippers tailored to their special requirements.

The shoes have to be tried out carefully. Some balance and break in correctly; some do not. It is unfortunate to discover the defects while on stage.

During the last century men's bodies have not changed appreciably except as the skeleton generally has grown taller and longer. The ballet technique for men has altered only to include extraordinary lifts and certain folk techniques. There has been no corresponding development to match the women's point work.

N. Y. Public Library Dance Collection, Roger Pryor Dodge Collection

Photo from "Le Ballet" by Boris Kochno and Maria Luz. Art du Monde. Hachette

Nijinsky in Giselle;

Opposite: Nijinsky in Les Orientales *and* Petrouchka

Diaghileff supplied Fokine with an unmatched company. The stars have become legends.

VASLAV NIJINSKY (1890-1950),

danseur noble, a practitioner of the classical or high style, who had fabulous elevation and pirouettes. He is by reputation the greatest jumper of all time. He could do six crossings of the legs in midair, that is, entrechat douze—twelve beats. George Washington Smith and Adeline Genée could do ten. No one has matched Nijinsky's feat. He used to rise into the air and "pause a little up there before he came down." Elevation was according to him a matter of breathing. Sarah Bernhardt said he was the greatest actor she had ever seen. Igor Stravinsky wrote: "To call him a dancer is not enough, for he was an even greater dramatic actor. His beautiful, but certainly not handsome, face could become the most powerful actor's mask I have ever seen and, as Petroushka, he was the most exciting human being I have ever seen on a stage." He choreographed four works—*Afternoon of a Faun*, still given on occasion; *Jeux;* the first, unsuccessful version of Stravinsky's *Le Sacre du Printemps;* and *Till Eulenspiegel,* music by Richard Strauss.

ANNA PAVLOVA (1881-1931)

Russian Jewess, daughter of a laundress and an unknown father, who brought beauty into more lives and carried inspiration further and with greater effect than any other single person in the history of the theater.

Anna Pavlova and Adolph Bolm made a trip through Scandinavia in 1905. She was the first ballerina to perform outside the confines of czarist Russia. Diaghileff's success in Paris the following years persuaded many of the stars to follow suit and to break with the Imperial Theatre. They thereby forfeited their pensions, titles, and positions. But directly there was a revolution and they found they'd lost nothing anyway and probably saved their necks.

Pavlova left the Diaghileff troupe after the first Paris season and, partnered by Mikhail Mordkin, formed her own company, a very enterprising and daring act. She toured on her own with changing partners for twenty years until her death. She traveled everywhere in the world that travel was possible, and introduced the ballet to millions who had never seen any form of Western dancing.

Her personal success everywhere was prodigious, but her repertoire was, on the whole, undistinguished. It consisted of versions of the old Russian works redone for her personal technique and style by her ballet master, Ivan Clustine. No new works of any excellence were created except two ravishing ballets by a young Hindu, Uday Shankar.

Her music and costumes were, for the most part, second-rate. She herself composed only two works, a solo for herself, *The California Poppy* with music inappropriately, but not surprisingly, by Tchaikowsky, and a ballet, *Autumn Leaves;* both poor.

Both photos on this page:
N. Y. Public Library Dance Collection, Roger Pryor Dodge Collection

Pavlova in The Swan.

Pavlova, St. Petersburg, 1906
N. Y. Public Library Dance Collection

150

Her most popular appearances were in two short dances by Michael Fokine: *The Dying Swan*—Saint-Saens (currently and marvelously performed by Maya Plisetskaya) and *The Autumn Bacchanale* by Glazounov; and two by Clustine, *The Pavlova Gavotte* and *The Dragonfly*. Her partners were Mikhail Mordkin, Alexander Volinine, Pierre Vladimiroff, Laurent Novikoff, and the American Hubert Stowitts.

One of her company's leading soloists was Muriel Stuart, who teaches in the School of the American Ballet; another was Edward Caton, teaching with Ballet Russe de Monte Carlo in New York.

With her long-limbed and racing body, she was the supreme exponent of the new style. She had the most beautiful foot in history, superb hands, and a deeply moving face.

Fokine wrote about her Mazurka in her first Paris appearance in *Les Sylphides*. "Pavlowa flew across the entire stage during the Mazurka. If one measured this flight in terms of inches, it actually would not be particularly high; many dancers jump higher. But Pavlowa's position in mid-air, her slim body—in short, her talent—consisted in her ability to create the impression not of jumping but of flying through the air. Pavlowa had mastered the difference between jumping and soaring, which is something that cannot be taught."

The poet Marianne Moore describes her extraordinary presence: "...the descending line of the propped forearm, of her dress and other hand, of ankle and foot, continues to the grass with the naturalness of a streamer of seaweed—an inevitable and stately serpentine which imparts to the seated figure the ease of a standing one.... We see her in the gavotte advancing with the swirling grace of a flag and the decorum of an impalla deer...the erectness of the head, the absolutely horizontal brows, indicating power of self-denial; the eyes, dense with imagination and sombered with solicitude; the hair, severely competent; the dress, dainty more than proud.... These truthful hands, the most sincere and the least greedy imaginable.... She had power for a most unusual reason—she did not present as valuable the personality from which she could escape."

In order to show off her marvelously slender legs, she shortened the ballet skirt to the abrupt tutu now currently in use. She had seen Isadora Duncan and she dared to be passionate. She had the gift of mass-hypnosis, a kind of magic. The only stars today with the same power of spell-binding are Galina Ulanova, Maya Plisetskaya, and the singer Maria Callas.

She moved fluidly without effort or block. She streamed; she flowed; she flamed. Her moments of stillness were a passionate quivering. Each gesture consumed the whole of her and carried her away like dying echoes. This was Diana, the huntress, a creature of the elements; one did not see body, one saw motion.

A generation of dancers turned to the art first because of her. She roused America as no one had done since Elssler. But she traveled farther and longer, making almost annual tours from coast to coast between 1912 and 1926. America became Pavlova-conscious and therefore ballet-conscious. She opened the last door. Dance and passion, dance and drama were thereafter fused.

From Haskell. "Picture History of Ballet." Studio Books

Pavlova dancing in her garden, Ivy House, London

La Fille Mal Gardée, c.1910

N. Y. Public Library Dance Collection

Karsavina in Les Sylphides

Mathilde Kschessinskaya
Le Théatre

Nijinska in Afternoon of a Faun

TAMARA KARSAVINA (1885-   ),

star of the Diaghileff company and the greatest actress of the ballet world. With her royal dark beauty and an intelligence supreme in the dance world, she served her art nobly. She created most of the immortal leads in the Fokine repertoire, giving them a personal stamp of theater-success which leave them among the most desirable roles in dance literature. "...the dancing in 'Les Sylphides' was especially suited to Karsavina's talent," wrote Fokine. "She did not possess either the slimness or the lightness of Pavlova, but in 'Les Sylphides' she demonstrated that rare romanticism which I seldom was able to evoke from other performers."

ADOLPH BOLM (1884-1951),

Pavlova's first great partner, a character dancer and actor, settled in America after World War I, choreographed for both the Metropolitan and Chicago Operas, and then founded his own school and ballet company, the Bolm Ballet Intime.

MATHILDE KSCHESSINSKAYA (1872-   ),

one of the two Prima Ballerinas Assoluta of the Imperial Ballet, an old-style star, the favorite of the Czar, later morganatic wife of the Grand Duke André, she was the controlling force in the Maryinsky Theatre. It was from the balcony of her palace that Lenin addressed the rioting mob in the October Revolution of 1917. She has since opened a ballet school in Paris and trained many of the leading dancers of the subsequent generations.

IDA RUBINSTEIN (1875-1961),

a very beautiful, slender woman, who was a fine mime. She was a rich woman of good family and was interested in dancing only as an amateur. She often performed the lead in *Schéhérazade*. Gabriele d'Annunzio and Claude Debussy created the ballet *St. Sébastien* for her. She later had her own company and commissioned the *Bolero* by Ravel, the music of which became an instantaneous international hit.

BRONISLAVA NIJINSKA (1890-   ),

Polish dancer and choreographer, the sister of Vaslav Nijinsky, created many of the roles in the early great Fokine works, and was, according to Stravinsky, the peer of her brother as a dancer. She is also what he was not—an original and witty choreographer even if with a manner somewhat dry and intellectual. She had none of the dramatic sweep and poignancy of Fokine, but because of the freshness of her approach, the delicacy and imagination of her handling of music, and the brightness of her satire, she has proved influential on other choreographers.

She continued to experiment with new music and expand the ballet techniques. She turned dancers' feet and knees in, and broke the rounded symmetrical design of their arms, going back to older and more primitive styles for inspiration. She also made experiments with jazz (but not tap). She is a remarkable teacher and coach, and one of the very few who remember first-hand the works and style of the pre-war, pre-Fokine Imperial Ballet.

LYDIA LOPOKOVA (1891-   ),

an adorable comedienne, splendid technician, the wife of the great economist John Maynard Keynes. As Lady Keynes, she has been one of the moving forces in the ballet renaissance in England and in the creation of the Royal Ballet.

LEONIDE MASSINE (1894-   ),

a brilliant dancer of demi-character, that is, not quite the high or noble style, but thoroughly schooled and splendid in technique, a first-class actor. He has unmatched rhythm; tremendous strength and spirit. His performance is always electric.

He succeeded Fokine and Nijinsky as master choreographer.

The stars of the later, post-war Diaghileff troupe were: Tamara Karsavina, Vera Nemchinova, Vera Trefilova, Felia Doubrovska, Alice Nikitina, Lydia Sokolova, Serge Lifar, Leon Woizikowski, Stanislas Idzikowsky, and Anton Dolin.

GEORGE BALANCHINE (1904-   ),

Russian dancer and choreographer, gave up performing early in his career for reasons of health and choreographic interest. He is the most prolific of all choreographers and, with the exception of Fokine, probably the most musical. An able pianist, he has even on occasion conducted. All his ballets are characterized by a masterly relation to the music.

He was an orthodox product of the St. Petersburg school until he unexpectedly widened his technique in vaudeville. It was under Diaghileff, however, that he found his first great style.

When revolution forced the young dancer and his wife, Tamara Geva, out of Russia in 1917, he sought employment in the popular music halls of Western Europe and was there exposed to types of work his elders had been protected from and which, under continuing Imperial conditions, he might never have seen.

At that time the variety and music halls in Europe and America were exploiting a kind of stunt dancing called acrobatic adage. The first famous practitioners were a French team, Mitti and Tillio. They were soon copied by troupes of boys and girls who climbed, tossed, hurled, slid, and threw one another all over the stage.

But even when the tricks worked, and notwithstanding the fact that they were always performed to music, the adage remained pure circus stunting. With great audacity, even hardihood, these performers invented remarkable lifts and holds, never dreamed of in classic ballet.

It was in the music halls that Balanchine learned the acrobatic stunts he later incorporated into the classic technique. Not since Carlotta Grisi's sensational fall from a cloud into the anxious arms of Petipa in *La Péri* had such daring been seen. Through his genius, the tossing, carrying, wrapping, and writhing found their way into meaningful design. He introduced these tricks first under the enterprising and open-minded sponsorship of Diaghileff.

Lopokova in Carnaval

Massine in Gaîté Parisienne

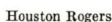

Today under his training the average corps de ballet dancer can achieve turns and batterie (beaten jumps), split leaps, and lifts barely within the compass of a ballerina in the pre-Diaghileff period. Technical virtuosity has come to be taken for granted.

The Bolshoi (Moscow) use many of these acrobatic lifts, throwings, and tossings with hair-raising effect, but with far less imagination and taste than Balanchine.

Balanchine made further revolutionary changes. He encouraged the use of bent knee on full and three-quarter point (first introduced by Nijinska) and the turned-in foot, positions absolutely counter to and forbidden by 19th-century classical dictates.

The innovations have endured.

Although himself so outstandingly musical, his demands on the dancers are mainly for physical precision.

They need little musicianship—only the ability to hear a downbeat and keep counting. Nor does he ask for acting ability. On the contrary, he tries to suppress all realistic show of emotion, even to the extent of erasing personality. Mime is reduced to a bare indication and the performer is urged to strive for anonymity and absence of personality. Balanchine is interested in the dancers only as tools, as a composer is interested in instruments.

One would think because of this that his ballets might be intellectual and dry. They are, on the contrary, deeply moving and exciting. This is due to composition alone, independent of interpretation. He can by means of rhythm and posture produce effects of great wit. There is, on the other hand, understandably little humor.

Balanchine was the last great choreographer to be developed by Diaghileff, and when Diaghileff died in 1929, an era ended and the members of his company scattered.

Leonide Massine was the only choreographer-performer with sufficient resilience to re-organize the veterans and their pupils into a successful unit of lasting achievement and creative force. It was due to his great talents that the revival of ballet took place and flourished in 1933-34. Among the children of Russian exiles in Paris he found an entirely new generation of young dancing stars. He continued the great Diaghileff tradition of using the best and freshest in the allied arts of music and design.

He attempted gigantic and serious works, sometimes to entire uncut symphonies, but his greatest achievements are the perfection of the variations scattered through his ballets, a brilliant development of the Petipa formula. He was also successful with bold mass movement and achieved remarkable sweeping effects.

He toured the United States for eight years (1934-42) and he did what Fokine himself had not been able to do, and what Pavlova had just begun: he roused America to the beauties and excitement of great ballet.

Massine and his finely mounted productions (Ballet Russe du Colonel de Basil) reached a vast audience. To large numbers he introduced Fokine's works properly done, excerpts of the Petipa masterpieces (seen for the first time in America) and his new exhilarating ones (the symphonic ballets, *Présages, Choreartium,* Beethoven's *Seventh*, Berlioz's *Symphonie Fantasque*, and *Beau Danube, Gaîté Parisienne,* and *Scuola di Ballo*) as well as fine samples of Nijinska and Balanchine performed most wonderfully by young, handsome, enthusiastic stars. There were many stars in his company and an absolutely dazzling array of soloists. He and Alexandra Danilova were the veteran leaders and he created leading roles in many of his own ballets.

The fine impression made by the initial season under the impresario Sol Hurok was cemented by seven subsequent cross-country trips. America was convinced at last. It liked ballet.

Concurrently with Massine, in 1934 Balanchine came to America at the behest of Lincoln Kirstein, and has been producing ballets more or less constantly since. He has to date composed nearly a round hundred pieces of varying length. His influence on the younger generation in this country is profound.

While keeping the style and shape of his pieces formal, Balanchine borrows colloquially the laced interweaving of American square dances, the acrobatics, stunts, and syncopations of our popular theater steps. He has in many ways taken on the coloring of new background but his so-called American pieces, *Western Symphony* (Hershey Kay), *Square Dance* (Vivaldi), and *Stars and Stripes* (Sousa-Kay) are European spoofs of popular American forms. They are highly amusing to people who know the forms intimately; they are neither authentic nor sympathetic treatments of authentic material. Despite his avowals, he remains abstract, and an apologist for the great Imperial tradition.

His link with Diaghileff's influence remains strong. He has re-adapted three of the classics and Fokine's *Firebird* in his own style. Because of his genius, the changes spell no deterioration. In his current repertory are his two great Diaghileff triumphs, *Apollo* and *The Prodigal Son*, the glory of the last Diaghileff season.

Unique among ballet composers, Balanchine has shown no falling off. He has good years and bad years, turning out five or six full-scale works a season, some trivial, some arresting and revolutionary. There is perceptible a steady growth, a deepening in emotional values. The Brahms *Liebeslieder Walzer* (1961) are perhaps the most exquisitely poignant lyric pieces of the century, excepting Fokine's *Sylphides*, but ranking with it in all ways.

Yvonne Mounsey and Francisço Monçion in Balanchine's The Prodigal Son

Balanchine's Liebeslieder Walzer *with Diana Adams and Bill Carter*

155

Ruth St. Denis in Radha, Paris, 1908

N. Y. Public Library Dance Collection, Denishawn Collection

The Revolutionists

INVENTION of new dance gesture, of a new way of moving, a new standard of line or coordination, is very rare. These matters develop slowly over generations. The most any ballet star or choreographer can hope to do is to expand or recombine what he has inherited. But during this century four women—Ruth St. Denis, Martha Graham, Mary Wigman, and Doris Humphrey—have invented really new dance movement, in the same way that Picasso invented new aesthetics and standards in painting.

Duncan, as we have seen, cut away all artificiality and made people remember the basics. She returned to childish, simple ways of running, walking, and skipping. She used the ground, she lay on it and sat on it. She used her arms and hands naturally, not in arbitrary movements of the 18th-century court.

RUTH ST. DENIS (1877-   ),

American dancer and choreographer, began a few years after Duncan to perform reproductions of the religious dances of India. She invented little, but she brought to the West poetic and moving examples of a very old art, and she reminded people that once men danced for religious purposes and that in large sections of the world many still do.

These were the first more or less authentic Eastern dances the West had seen. Before this, Oriental dancing, with the undulating hips, vibrating shoulders, and wiggling arms of partly naked dancers (bare stomach and ribs, in the case of women; bare torso, in the case of men) seemed highly improper. Any practitioners who came up from Africa or the Near East were frankly girls of low morals who performed in dives for customers who did not have art particularly on their minds. St. Denis' integrity was beyond question; no one in his wildest dreams could think her intentions anything but pure.

There had been Oriental ballets before, such as *Bayadère* (performed by Taglioni) and *La Péri* (by Grisi), but these were done in tutus, on point, and from a most superficial and theatric point of view. St. Denis gave us the real thing without, however, using native music. She danced to Western pieces, romantically composed under Oriental influence, and performed on Western instruments. She was a sensational success and had many imitators and followers.

She also taught. With her husband, Ted Shawn (1891-   ), she founded a school in Los Angeles, Denishawn, where dancing was practiced in conjunction with related arts and philosophies. According to Baird Hastings in *The Denishawn Era*, this was "the first serious school of the dance [in America] with a curriculum and a standard of achievement."

St. Denis and Shawn attracted great pupils. Boys and girls of education and serious purpose began to study. These were the first American men in this century to interest themselves in any dancing besides tap and ballroom. These were the first girls from "good families" to study professionally.

Martha Swope

Martha Swope

skirt, tight sweater, and leather pouch, was the type established by the Graham dancer. The straight, dark, long-skirted costume and the leotard, replacing the ballet tutu or folk dress, were her invention. The accepted work uniform today for all dancers, ballet and modern, has become the Graham leotard. The American ballet students wear it with traditional tights and point shoes, and the European is gradually adopting it also. No ballet student anywhere now works in tutu and bloomers. The leotard has become ubiquitous in civil life.

Graham dancers are the reverse of frivolous and coquettish. They were, like the Denishawn pupils, educated people. Many have become teachers in American universities. Several have become good choreographers: Anna Sokolow, Pearl Lang, Jean Erdman, Sophie Maslow, John Butler, and Paul Taylor.

Historically speaking, Graham has had as forceful an impact on all branches of the contemporary theater as Duncan. Technically, in terms of invented and added steps and style, hers is the greatest single life contribution in the records of dancing. Her dance dramas compare with the work of our greatest playwrights.

In the words of William Schuman, the composer and president of the Lincoln Center for the Performing Arts at the ninth annual Capezio Dance Award Luncheon honoring Martha Graham:

"She has created an original vocabulary of dance movement that has added a new dimension to the expressivity of the choreographic art.

Barbara Morgan Photo from "Martha Graham" by B. Morgan, pub. Duell, Sloan & Pearce

Martha Graham
in Primitive Mysteries, *1930*

Pearl Lang

Peter Basch

"She has been gloriously incapable, ever, of being slight, captious or superficial. Her works—whether tragic or comic—always probe, distill, and illuminate.

"She continues to create with undiminished zeal. Each new work brings the excitement of discovery of previously unexplored facets of her endlessly fertile imagination.

"For these reasons she has achieved a position which is not adequately to be described solely as one of pre-eminence in her field. For whether we speak of the world of Dance, of Music, of Literature, or of the Graphic Arts, Martha Graham is one of the greatest artists America has ever produced."

Graham maintains a school in New York and teaches master courses at Connecticut College every summer. She cannot tour through this country because of mounting union costs, so her annual short spring season in New York is the object of pilgrimages from all over the Americas. Her present company in points of execution, style, and finesse of presentation places her theater on a par with the great historic companies—with the Diaghileff troupe in its heyday and with the Grand Kabuki of Japan. It is unquestionably the most stylish theater we have evolved and should be taken over by the government and preserved as the basis for an enduring national institution.

Only three of her works have been filmed. None is yet Labanotated. The bulk of this great repertory is in danger of loss. It constitutes a national treasure. It should be our prime duty to preserve it. Now. While there is still time.

MARY WIGMAN (1886-   ),

German dancer and choreographer, concurrently with Graham experimented in Germany on many of the same problems. She studied with the innovator Rudolph von Laban, but surpassed him and all her colleagues in achievement. She discovered new ways of moving, the ebb and flow of motion, *"Spannung und Entspannung,"* the expansion of power and its release.

Like Graham she used the floor and danced barefoot. She avoided all balletic postures, though she used the turned-out thigh and foot—as do most dance techniques—for the simple reason that it always provides the best basis for balance.

She was fascinated by movement as organic pattern, the development of visual conclusions and enlargements from single gestures or simple phrases of gesture. No one before had analyzed and exposed movement as material capable of all the treatments, developments, and variations that melody and harmony are subject to.

Wigman subordinated music, very nearly discarding it altogether, using only percussive instruments, gongs, drums, wood blocks after the style of primitives. The dances and the rhythmic accompaniment were developed together. This method insured an independent and strong dance form, one that did not lean on the music for emotional meaning. Wigman examined each step for its strength or weakness, without the encouragement of melody. She placed gongs and drums in the dancer's hand. She employed platforms, and levels became part of the patterns. She stressed visual rhythm, visual development rather than pose or brilliance of tricks.

Her costumes were simple, an abstraction of Asian skirt and choli, or the Asian woman's trousers. She was always barefooted or in sandals; she never used the arched foot or point work.

Her subject matter was largely abstract or based on semi-religious celebrations, rites, and festivals, and she brought to all she did an aura of ritualistic dedication. She was less dramatic and more symbolic than Graham. She projected an air of universality.

She was a German and therefore philosophic, systematic, analytic, and articulate. She wrote and taught, and many, many people wrote about her in all languages. An entire system of composing and training was based on her method. She was a very great teacher and pupils came from all over the world to her schools in Dresden, Berlin, and Stuttgart. When they returned to their own countries they spread her gospel. Among her most famous pupils were Vera Skoronel, Harald Kreutzberg, and Yvonne Georgi (choreographer and ballet master for the Hanover Opera), Margaret Wallmann (no longer a choreographer but a leading director of the Scala), and Hanya Holm (now a Broadway choreographer). From Wigman stems an entire epoch.

Under the Hitler regime, the schools broke up and changed hands. Refugees scattered everywhere. Wigman is now back in West Berlin teaching in her own school. Occasionally she choreographs for the Staatsoper there; her own company is disbanded.

The point of view of Graham and Wigman was in many ways similar although their technical inventions differed. They had

S. Enkelman from Private Collection of Hanya Holm

Mary Wigman

Harald Kreutzberg

S. Enkelmann

The Green Table by Kurt Jooss

Doris Humphrey

Marcus Blechman

N. Y. Public Library Dance Collection

read about each other but had never met. Neither had seen any of the other's work before maturing in her own art. It was spontaneous response to contemporary influences on opposite sides of the Atlantic. This happens sometimes in science and often in art.

The influence of Wigman in central Europe has been widespread and lasting. There is an established School of Central European Movement with a technique and style all its own. Some of its chief exponents are distinguished choreographers, and the heads of great institutions.

The most notable of these is Kurt Jooss (1901-   ), pupil of von Laban, founder of Ballets Jooss, and choreographer in chief at the Essen Opera. He has composed several masterpieces. The most famous is *The Green Table* (music by Frederick Cohen). A number of his pupils went to South America during World War II and established companies of modern dance in Chile, Peru, Argentina, and Venezuela.

DORIS HUMPHREY (1895-1958),

American dancer and choreographer, a pupil of Ruth St. Denis and Ted Shawn, became one of the greatest native choreographers. Her impact on American dancing has been felt more through compositions and teachings than through technical developments. Her dance style continued the pseudo-Greek expression of Denishawn, employing floating gesture based on breath control and light, fleet foot movements.

She used levels very much in the style of Mary Wigman, and danced to music of all kinds, classic and modern, also dramatic and expressive sounds like humming, shouting, buzzing.

She taught the whole of her adult life, influencing and guiding two generations of professional pupils. For twenty years she maintained with Charles Weidman a school and performing company in New York City. After the dissolution of this school, she taught at the Young Men's Hebrew Association and the Juilliard School of Music. She is the only master ever to teach dance composition as a fine art in America. She has written one of the four great treatises on the subject, The Art of Making Dances, published posthumously in 1959.

Her pupils have been extraordinarily creative. Alone of all great choreographers, she released individuality instead of cramping it. José Limón and Sybil Shearer have developed personal styles that are in no sense rubber stamp versions of hers.

Her output from 1920 to 1958 was prolific and she was always courageous in the use of fresh themes, new untried music, and inventive stage effects.

Graham, Wigman, and Humphrey stressed the development of gesture according to its own internal rhythm, independent of musical phrase and beat. The subject matter of their work is always serious, not necessarily tragic, but thoughtful and searching.

These five pioneers—Duncan, St. Denis, Wigman, Graham, Humphrey—founded their own schools and maintained their own companies and traditions. They were, none of them, state-endowed. Wigman, it is true, had state help for a short period before she fell into disfavor with the Nazis, but for most of her life she has had to support her own work.

The pupils these women attracted were mature, and came through choice. They were not sent by their parents, nor indentured to the state when young, as in the old opera ballet companies. They came the way apprentices come to great painters. The new technique, the style and the compositions were worked out together, master and pupil struggling with the same problems. The performers were rarely paid and had to work for their living at menial jobs, such as waiting on tables in restaurants. They gave their whole time, their strength and their youth to the formation of these techniques with no great hope of personal advancement and no guarantee of performing careers.

They asked merely to serve the art form and their chosen masters. It takes a serious and dedicated human being to do this, and the modern dancer of the thirties and forties was in point of view less like a ballet dancer of the preceding centuries and more like a dancing acolyte, or a Renaissance craftsman. These girls and boys and their leaders pulled their profession back into dignity, into the respect of other artists, and into acceptance by the community.

Dancing as a profession is now permitted; in America still, less to men than to women, but permitted. Wherever dancing is part of the religious and communal life, it is accepted as an art quite normally—where it is not, it is reserved for the outcasts and misfits. The sheer caliber of the modern performer and his serious attitude are gradually changing what has unfortunately been the American attitude.

It is interesting that five of the greatest rebels against tradition have been women, and that four of them were Americans.

Marcus Blechman

Doris Humphrey in Chorale Prelude

Jose Limon

Peterich

The Traditional European Ballet Students

1. There are as many boys as girls.

2. They come of a poor or lower class family.

3. They are young.

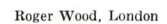

4. Their parents choose their careers. Choosing the dancing academy is simple—there is only one, a state school or branches of it. (Except in Paris where there are several famous teachers.)

5. They have no education beyond what the state school gives them, but this is excellent in language, history, music, and the arts.

6. On graduation they will be assured of a competence and, on retirement, of a pension.

7. They want fame and fortune. They consider dance a good profession and they are grateful for the opportunity to embrace it because otherwise they might be working on a farm or in a factory.

8. Their path was charted long ago.

9. Very few of them have creative gifts.

All of this is true of the American ballet student except that they have none of the benefits of state school or government, and their education is no more and no less than what is enforced by American law.

164

Her rhythm, visual and audible in castanets and feet were unmatched. In fact, no one since has approached her in the architecture of the solo Spanish dance. During her life, she was accused of departing from authentic tradition, and she did, as Mozart and Beethoven departed from German folk tunes. She made tradition. She left tradition enriched. Classic Spanish dancing is now accepted the world over as the elegant and subtle peer of any form of theater dance.

VINCENTE ESCUDERO (1889-   )

A flamenco or gypsy dancer, a great artist and brilliant theater man, choreographed short but finely fashioned dances for himself and his small troupe. For sixty years he has been a dominant figure on the Spanish scene.

ARGENTINITA (1898-1945)

Less creative and more orthodox than Argentina, but the charming head of a first-class troupe. She was the first to treat South and Central American folk forms creatively. Edwin Denby says, "...Argentinita's dances had a charmingly ladylike air, with no athletics and no heroics. Sometimes the steps and patterns seemed naively plain and the best ones were never very elaborate, but her group numbers were always completely transparent and their comedy points rarely failed to register....Her own manner of dancing...was completely graceful, completely defined and her rhythm was infallible. Her special glory as a dancer were her little slippered feet, in their tiny, airy dartings and in their pretty positions on the floor."

There have been many excellent Spanish groups since, those of Teresita, La Joselito, Pilar Lopez, Mariemma, Carmen Amaya, Antonio and Rosario, Roberto Iglesias, to name a few. The trends and styles of their work have not materially departed from the models set and defined by the illustrious three described above.

HELBA HUARA

A Peruvian dancer—composed dramatic solos in the Spanish and South American idioms and performed them here in the late twenties. Her technique was splendid, her creative invention and emotional power unforgettable. Blindness cut short what might have been a tremendously influential career.

CARMELITA MARACCI (1911-   )

An important creative talent in this field, if little known. A California girl, Spanish-trained, she boasts a phenomenal ballet technique in addition to fine castanet and heel work. She is a true original, a satirist, a composer in the grand line, one of the great American choreographers. Her solo compositions are among this century's best, but her influence has unhappily been restricted because of infrequent performing due to ill health. "The terrain I traveled," says Maracci, "was not the studio floor, for my world led me into Goya's land of terror and blood-soaked pits....The life

Collection of Lillian Moore

Vincente Escudero

Carmelita Maracci

Edward Weston/Courtesy of Carmelita Maracci

I lived could not make me a dancer of fine dreams and graveyard decor... so I danced hard about what I saw and lived. I was not an absentee landlord; I was one of the dispossessed. I was a gypsy joad."

UDAY SHANKAR (1902-   )

Hindu dancer who served his apprenticeship in Anna Pavlova's company, choreographing for her two exquisite ballets. He built a troupe of native dancers and musicians and toured the world several times. His dances are not strictly authentic, but somewhat theatricalized in the Western sense. He possesses, however, impeccable taste, and he has done much to make the dances of his country understandable to, and beloved by, Westerners.

He founded a school on a site in India presented to him by the government. He is the first Asian to attempt contemporary subject matter and gestures in the traditional idiom, achieving modernism without ever becoming Western.

KATHERINE DUNHAM (1914-   )

American dancer and choreographer. The first person to organize a Negro troupe of concert caliber and explore the rich folklore of her race. In studies of the United States urban forms, the Caribbean types (Cuban, Haitian, and Jamaican), and certain African derivations, she proved herself not only an anthropologist of note but a consummate theater artist.

A delicious performer, she manifests that rarest of all combinations, lyric beauty, eroticism, and humor. She has infused her

Uday Shankar

Uday Shankar and his wife

Moiseyev dancers

company with a flare for characterization and atmosphere rarely equaled. She pioneered in a difficult field, cutting away from all traditional clichés and presenting the Negro in fresh, astute, and delicately observed moods.

The physical difficulties of her endeavor were enormous, since the housing and travel conditions she met with in her own country presented unending handicaps and prejudices. She faced them head on and overcame them. Her name is now internationally known.

There are other Negro art dance groups (Asadata Dafora, Pearl Primus, Geoffrey Holder from Trinidad, Alvin Ailey and Carmen de Lavallade, Lavenia Williams in Haiti). Many of Dunham's pupils have been integrated into established companies, Martha Graham's and the New York City Center Ballet Company, to name two. Dunham was the first to set the example by founding a school, training dancers, and offering sustained opportunity for performance under dignified conditions.

IGOR MOISEYEV (1906-   )

Russian choreographer whose work has furnished the West with the finest examples of contemporary Soviet choreography. While most of his dances are short pieces, his folk compositions are striking and often poignantly moving. The technique of his large troupe is unexampled and its success has been uniformly great

Katherine Dunham

wherever it has appeared. Moiseyev's genius lies in the rhythmic development of geometric pattern, and in the emotional impact of formal symmetric figurations in space. They rely for effect on the numbers employed, the perfection of execution, and the magic of sequence. This is what lifts them to art and away from the displays of gymnasts and music hall lines. But the patterns are unsophisticated in the extreme except in their aggregate effect.

THE UKRAINIAN BALLET

This robust group headed by its founder and choreographer, Pavel Virsky, boasts the usual Soviet quota of flabbergasting male technicians and several dozen pretty but undifferentiated females. The dances are, for the most part, charming and exuberant though inferior in structure and style to those of the Moiseyev troupe. The *Embroiderers,* a Ukrainian round dance in which the girls weave intricate patterns with ribbon streamers, the Cossack *Spear Dance,* and *The New Boots* are supremely effective.

THE INBAL COMPANY OF ISRAEL

This company was organized and directed by Sara Levi-Tanai (Israeli)—a true pioneer who in ten years has built an art theater of singers and dancers that ranks with the best. She does more than revive folk forms, for the folk forms of her country were lost or corrupted. She has re-created a style and invented composition of real power. The members of her company are first-class actors and sing as well as dance.

Mme. Levi-Tanai composes much of the music for her pieces.

THE BAYHANYHAN-PHILIPPINO FOLK DANCE COMPANY

This group of student-amateurs, trained and sponsored by the Philippine Women's University of Manila, has done excellent pioneering work in the reviving of all types of native dances from the primitive Igorot through the Moro (Mohammedan) of Mindanao, and from the Spanish colonial to the many contemporary rustic types.

The performance level is simple but good, the music and costume research superb. The company is fortunate in having a choreographer of real gifts in Lucrezia Urtulla, and a manager of genius in Helena Benitez.

In less than a decade the troupe has established a world reputation. With the resources of the university always available, it promises to become a lasting national institution.

KOLO (The Yugo-Slav State Company)

comes from Serbia. It was organized in 1948 by Olga Skovran and its permanent home is in Belgrade. It is entirely subsidized by the state through the Ministry of Education. The dances represented are Serbian, Crotian, Slovenian, Montenegrin, and Macedonian. They are rich, vigorous and beautiful and reflect traditional influences from Turkish, Hungarian, and Greek heritage.

Bayhanyhan-Philippino Dance Company

Kolo, the Yugo-Slav State Company

Ballet Folklorico: Dolores Castillo and Armand Medina

The troupe is of high professional caliber, particularly notable in the beauty and strength of the male dancing; in Olga Skovran it is blessed with a choreographer of vivid dramatic instinct.

SLASK (Polish State Folk Ballet)

Founded in 1953 by Stanislav Hadyna, who acts as managing director. Its choreographer and ballet mistress is Elmira Kaminska. It is state supported.

BALLET FOLKLORICO DE MEXICO

Under the direction of Amalia Hernandez, this is a large group of young and handsome dancers which has had considerable popularity in Mexico City and won the international prize for folk companies in Paris, 1961. It reproduces the rich and varied styles in an old and beautiful culture. The costumes are superb and the music is authentic, with complete orchestras of instruments and singers from each province.

BALLET POPULAR DE MEXICO

Similar to the Folklorico except that it boasts the exceptional choreographic gifts of Guillermo Arriaga, who besides his incomparable folk reproductions composes effectively in the modern style. Unlike the more fortunate, larger company, the Ballet Popular is not state supported.

THE AZUMA KABUKI THEATRE

This company carries a repertory of capsule versions of the plays and dances of the Grand Kabuki Theatre, clarified and shortened for Western understanding but with no loss of style or poignancy. Such translation represents a miracle of taste on the part of the choreographer, Fujima. His widow, Mme. Azuma, a member of the great theatrical dynasty, stars in the troupe which departs from tradition in allowing women to play classic as well as contemporary roles. The costumes and decor, as in all classic Japanese theater, are supremely beautiful. The music is native and well played.

Fujima's tragic death is a great artistic loss. His theater, and ours, could use his taste, integrity, and happy invention, as well as his deep scholarship. He was an artist and a showman and, what is rare in the Orient, one who was willing to depart from tradition and experiment without any slavish acceptance of Western clichés.

In the last fifty years there have been a number of mimes and clowns who have worked with effect, composing their own vehicles, and maintaining on occasion their own companies. Among them must be listed Rita Sachetto (Austrian), Colette Willy (French—later better known as a novelist under the name of Colette), Alexander Sakharoff (Russian), Angna Enters (American), Trudi Schoop (Swiss), Lotte Goslar (German), Agnes de Mille (American), Marcel Marceau (French). All of them have had influence on their contemporaries.

Hurok

Fujima

Both photographs of Fujima N. Y. Public Library Dance Collection

Statuette of Galina Ulanova

Martha Swope

Contemporary Ballet

THE Diaghileff Ballet Russe was the first great company to try to make its way without state or royal support. Its annual deficit was met by gifts from private millionaires, among others Lady Cunard, Lady Ripon, Gabrielle Chanel, the couturière, the Aga Khan, and Otto Kahn, a rich American who helped support the Metropolitan Opera.

With the breakdown of monarchies after World War I, stars began to build their own companies, seeking aid wherever they could get it. These companies were necessarily dependent on one or at most several box-office personalities, and therefore were comparatively short-lived and of variable fortune and location. Dancers with no fixed allegiance, or even nationality (there were two generations of displaced White Russian dancers after the Bolshevik Revolution) rushed about from troupe to troupe carrying their traditions and techniques with them, and sowing interest and knowledge wherever they went. Whenever, during the last fifty years, a choreographer failed to find an opening in an established troupe, he straightway set about building his own company. Such a proceeding would have been unthinkable in earlier times.

These smaller companies, maintained by stars, had no official status and have made their way by touring, without state or civic support. Most of them endured only a decade or two. None of them lasted past the life of the organizer. In a few instances good ballet or fine scores were produced that found their way into more permanent repertoires. Among these companies must be listed the troupes of Anna Pavlova, Adolph Bolm, Ida Rubinstein, Jean Borlin (Ballets Suédois), Catherine Littlefield (Philadelphia Ballet), Mia Slavenska and Frederic Franklin, and Mikhail Mordkin.

Today there are two or three dozen ballet troupes functioning in Europe and the Americas, among them, the Festival Ballet of Anton Dolin, the Chicago Opera of Ruth Page, the San Francisco Opera of Lew and William Christensen, the Western Ballet of England, the Royal Winnipeg, the Royal Canadian (Toronto), Les Ballets Canadiens (Montreal), and the companies of Roland Petit, Janine Charrat, Jerome Robbins, Herbert Ross, Robert Joffrey, John Butler, Zachary Solov, and Agnes de Mille.

The contributions of these troupes have been in some instances history-making, but the well-being of the art depends on the large and enduring companies.

Ballet has shown the least decadence in Denmark, the greatest creativity in England and America.

For seventy-five years, the great ballet centers of France, Italy, Germany and Austria have been, artistically speaking, dormant. The opera ballets of Germany and Austria declined before World War I and were taken over in the twenties by the followers of Wigman and Von Laban. Ballet technique was discarded; the entire classic repertory was lost or redone in modern movement. There were, for instance, versions of *Coppélia* off-point—flatfooted in Middle-European plastique. Since the war there has been a tendency to revert to the original versions, but this has meant building up ballet schools from scratch. Some of these new works are fine, like the operas and ballets of Essen under the direction of

Kurt Jooss, The Berlin Staats Oper flourishes under the expert leadership of Tatiana Gsovsky and Mary Wigman who is invited in for special occasions. But it is Stuttgart, as in the time of Noverre, which once more leads Europe. It has imported John Cranko of the Royal Ballet and is now producing operas and ballets of the highest excellence.

Italy and Belgium have produced well-trained dancers but nothing of creative interest in eighty years.

The French people are irrepressible, but not in the Opéra; the Opéra stagnates. For three decades it has been under the choreographic leadership of foreigners, and not always the best. The Opéra's wisest decisions were to persuade Balanchine to come from America for a short season, and Harald Lander to come from Denmark. These two produced beautiful and effective pieces.

For a long time the emphasis in this great house, the master house of ballet, has been placed on superficial spectacles, on dress making and decoration, while the choreography, the heart of the business, remains derivative, empty and bloodless.

The French genius operates in the smaller companies that mushroom up in Paris from time to time, producing works of extraordinary effectiveness. It is ironic that the young independent creative artists were nearly all pupils of the Opéra, Roland Petit (1924-   ), Janine Charrat (1924-   ), and Jean Babilée (1923-   ), but it is outside the great national lyric theater that they function.

The other large French company, the Grand Ballet du Marquis de Cuevas, now defunct and dancers scattered, was formed in 1944 in America with American money, but for the last fifteen years it established its home bases in Monte Carlo and Paris. This was a big troupe with a cosmopolitan and changing complement of choreographers and dancers. It traveled exclusively in Europe, South America, and the Near East. It produced a great number of works, of which only a very few are likely to endure.

Russia, which led the ballet world from 1885 to 1914, finds itself in a strange and unprecedented state.

Two generations of its greatest artists left just before and after the revolution. These scattered all over the earth, but chiefly in Europe and America. There was a numerous colony of white Russians taught by the exiled Prima Ballerina Assoluta, Mathilde Kschessinskaya, now living in Paris, and the other great historic ladies, Egorova, Trefilova, Préobrajenska. The children they instructed were to form the nucleus of the new ballet groups, three of these organized in 1933-34 by former associates of the late Serge Diaghileff.

These companies must be discussed as a unit, because of their internecine character. Their contribution was a great one: the preservation of seven of the Fokine classics, the creation of the bulk of Massine's work, as well as important new pieces by Fokine, Nijinska, Balanchine, Lichine, Ashton, and de Mille.

During the decade, 1933-1943, the creativity of the various branches of the Monte Carlo Ballets Russe (Col. de Basil, René Blum, Sergei Denham) was amazing and in influence has proven

Baron Studios

Renée Jeanmaire and Roland Petit in Petit's Carmen

Nathalie Philippart and Jean Babilée in Babilée's L'Amour et son Amour

Courtesy of American Ballet Theatre

173

*Ludmila Bogomolova and
Stanislav Vlasov in* Spring Waters

John G. Ross

second only to that of the Diaghileff troupe. The chief support came first from the Prince of Monaco, who gave them a home and a theater, and later, during the war, from the American Julius Fleischman. They traveled the world over. They made nine consecutive tours through England and the United States and aroused interest in dancing to a degree unknown before. No matter how violent the competition between companies, the chief functions remained constant:

a) The production of great new ballets.

b) Missionary work in England and America—in the thirties these two countries at last converted and the English and American native ballet were as a consequence born.

The home companies of Mother Russia, left behind by the sudden departure of so many brilliant sons and daughters, a whole chapter of their creative life erased, laboring under heavy state supervision, have preserved what was easiest to preserve: the physical body of the technique. But creatively they have fallen into a strange and prolonged trance. The Soviet ballet is in truth "The Sleeping Beauty."

The Soviet ballet now comprises many organizations and schools, but its classic wing is still divided, as it was under the Czar, into the two main branches, Leningrad and Moscow, and the 19th-century traditions and characteristics have been largely maintained. "St. Petersburg was the city of court and art," says Alexandra Danilova, "Moscow, the city of merchants. It was a peasant town without taste or culture except what was reflected in great private collections." This divergence in interest and background was reflected in the two great branches of the Imperial Ballet School. Under imperial patronage, both schools trained boys and girls from early childhood, maintained theaters, toured companies, and pensioned their veterans. These schools and theaters and traditions have been taken over bodily by the Soviets with no appreciable change in point of view, organization, or training.

The basic differences in style developed during the 19th century between St. Petersburg and Moscow still prevail. The Maryinsky at St. Petersburg (or currently the Kirov State Academic Theatre of Opera and Ballet at Leningrad) stressed quietness, restraint, brilliance with discipline, body line, musicality. The Moscow School emphasized athleticism, tours de force, stunting, endurance, and abandoned vigor. The Maryinsky graduated Mathilde Kschessinskaya, Lubov Egorova, Vera Trefilova, Anna Pavlova, Vaslav Nijinsky, Mikhail Mordkin, Michael Fokine, and be it noted, the most spiritual member of the Bolshoi (Moscow) troupe, Galina Ulanova. The Moscow boasted Ekaterina Geltzer, Adolph Bolm, Asaf Messerer, Maya Plisetskaya, and Raisa Struchkova.

The Moscow style permits a flamboyant use of the arms and hands, an extra bending of the back, a swooping and twisting and waving, too lush for more Western liking. The Moscow School seems to overstate. The Danish, English, and American companies perform with greater sparseness and economy. They cherish simplicity in line and attack. The lavish use of Moscow wrist, fingers, rippling elbow joints and backs we would not tolerate here. And in

Moscow they have neglected the careful precision of footwork for great jumps. The Italian influence has all but been erased. Their dancers nevertheless please vast audiences. It is a matter of differing taste. And it must be noted with interest that after their tours of the West and consequent first exposure to Western taste, they modified their extravagances while preserving their fantastic virtuosity. Maya Plisetskaya's *Dying Swan*, while unlike anything technically permissible here, is one of the great theatre experiences of our time.

Due to the dancers' physical virtuosity and opulence of production, the popularity of the Bolshoi troupe wherever they go is overwhelming. They have changed the classics *Swan Lake* and *Aurora's Wedding* almost beyond recognition, although their *Giselle* is still extremely beautiful and traditional.

But by world standards, the Bolshoi has not produced a single new ballet (excepting Messerer's *Ballet Class*) that can meet the best choreographic qualifications established and practiced else-

Swan Lake, Act 3: Nicolai Fadeyechev and Maya Plisetskaya

where, nor any decor that can compete with good modern design. Given every physical help, they have failed to develop the one essential necessary to the growth of an art—free imagination.

The great creative impulses in contemporary ballet have come from England and America.

In the 19th century, London knew no lack of great dancers, but they were all visitors. A belief persisted that the English had not the temperament nor the stamina to make dancing stars. There were various ballet schools run by French and Italian masters, but no national company and no free experiment as in America.

In 1909 the Russians began filtering in—first Lydia Kyasht who danced at the Empire Theater, then Karsavina at the Coliseum, then Anna Pavlova and Mikhail Mordkin, and finally Diaghileff. England took them all to her heart. Pavlova, Karsavina, Kyasht, Lopokova, and the beloved Danish star, Adeline Genée, made this city their permanent legal home. Four of them married Englishmen. The Diaghileff troupe traveled a great deal but returned annually to London and its cheering audiences.

There was an active, enthusiastic, and knowledgeable ballet public clamoring for a ballet, and still no native company. In answer to this need two women of genius stepped forward. Neither of them, curiously, was English; one was Irish, the other Polish.

THE BALLET CLUB OR BALLET RAMBERT

In 1929 a group calling themselves The Camargo Society produced a series of small concerts with choreography by Marie Rambert, Ninette de Valois, and Frederick Ashton. Their efforts met with insufficient support to continue, but Rambert (a former pupil of Cecchetti) founded a school and a minute theater in what had been a church vestry house. She organized Sunday night performances for club members. The young people she brought together, and the impact of their work, were of such importance as to have proved a shaping influence on our century's theater. She provided rehearsal studios and a theater when none was available for untried native talent; she provided experienced supervision, taste, and farsightedness. She unquestionably broke down the Englishman's prejudice against English dancing and proved in front of their eyes that the British boys and girls could hold their own with any in the world. She ushered in the renaissance in ballet dancing that has made England lead the world. She did this with a long-range plan and daily discipline that did not waver in taste or exactitude.

Rambert introduced the work of Frederick Ashton, Antony Tudor, Andrée Howard, Frank Staff, Walter Gore, and William Mourice, and put a stage under Alicia Markova's feet when there was none elsewhere.

Ballet Club, now called The Ballet Rambert, still functions. It has made extensive tours through the Middle and Far East and Australia. In 1959 it visited America. Two pupils have established ballet companies across the world—Celia Franca (the Royal Canadian) in Toronto, and Peggy van Praagh in Australia.

Marie Rambert was created Dame of the British Empire in 1962.

Walter Gore's Simple Symphony

Marie Rambert

Houston Rogers